Customer Relationship Management

Springer
Berlin
Heidelberg
New York
Hong Kong
London
Milan
Paris
Tokyo

Federico Rajola

Customer Relationship Management

Organizational and Technological Perspectives

With 37 Figures and 13 Tables

 Springer

Professor Dr. Federico Rajola
Università Cattolica del Sacro Cuore
Largo Gemelli, 1
20123 Milan
Italy
federico.rajola@unicatt.it

ISBN 3-540-44001-1 Springer-Verlag Berlin Heidelberg New York

Cataloging-in-Publication Data applied for
A catalog record for this book is available from the Library of Congress.
Bibliographic information published by Die Deutsche Bibliothek
Die Deutsche Bibliothek lists this publication in the Deutsche Nationalbibliografie; detailed bibliographic data is available in the Internet at <http://dnb.ddb.de>.

Springer-Verlag Berlin Heidelberg New York
a member of BertelsmannSpringer Science+Business Media GmbH

http://www.springer.de

© Springer-Verlag Berlin · Heidelberg 2003
Printed in Germany

Hardcover-Design: Erich Kirchner, Heidelberg

SPIN 10887941   42/3130-5 4 3 2 1 0 – Printed on acid-free paper

To my son Alessandro

Acknowledgements

The author would like to express his thanks to all those who assisted him with the conception of this book, in particular to CeTIF and its research community, Mauro Bello, Rita Bissola, Alberto Boffi, Chiara Frigerio, Vanessa Gemmo and Francesco Virili, for their helpful and interesting comments at various stages of development of the present work.

Special gratitude is due to Marco De Marco, Andrea Carignani and Cecilia Rossignoli, who offered helpful suggestions throughout the project.

Particular thanks go to Karin Lanzer for her support in reviewing and proofreading the manuscript, for her competent and friendly assistance, and her incredible patience in collecting and organizing all the comments and suggestions that came up throughout the writing process.

Thanks to Paolo Arosio for his invaluable technical assistance, which has made it possible to enhance the printed word with appropriate graphics.

Many thanks to all those who have enthusiastically supported the author's efforts from start to finish. Hopefully all of them will be pleased to see that all their efforts have now come to fruition.

Contents

Introduction

Many authors have studied CRM from a technological perspective, while others have focused their work on management issues. This book intends to study the phenomena from an organizational and technological perspective, focusing on the relevant actions to be carried out in a CRM project. The purpose is also to use an organizational framework to explain the fundamentals of CRM initiatives. As described in the text, CRM is not only a technological matter, but above all an organizational one, and it is important to define change management activities to support it.

Nowadays we are seeing more and more articles, special issues of journals, scientific books, and conferences on such themes as Business Intelligence and CRM and their introduction into firms. Can this be considered a sign that firms now have a real interest in systems that allow decision processes to be managed in better ways?

This probably is the case. While these technologies, used today for customer management, have already been available, and even well established, for some decades, it was previously considered that they were for the exclusive use of "boffins".

So who are these boffins? They are people considered to be geniuses, who live in a special dimension and who study and work on subjects, technologies and abstract theories that are hardly applicable to concrete business initiatives.

After some years, Business Intelligence and CRM boffins took their revenge. They demonstrated that these technologies could have concrete applications in business initiatives and might even help management to achieve competitive advantages.

But was it just a technological problem? Are firms ready to adapt systems that are sometimes invasive and often require enforcement of a radical cultural business change? Why do more than 50% of Business Intelligence and CRM projects not culminate in the expected results?

The facts are surely more complex than they appear. The contribution of Business Intelligence and CRM systems to the achievement of a competitive advantage requires:

- A real alignment between technology and business objectives,

- Full integration with legacy systems that have been adapted for years, in order to support business transactions,

- Integration between DSSs (Decision Support Systems) that have been conceived on the initiative of single users. These often produce data and information that are not properly aligned with the business information system.

- A better understanding of business transactions, so that the increasing competition can be managed,

- Planning of technological initiatives, so that irrational interventions in this field can be avoided.

  This should lead to an architectural model that induces improvement in all decisional processes. A further positive effect should be the systematization of technologies available on the market, in order to avoid cases of adaptation induced by imitative intentions.

- Proper training of users in the use of Business Intelligence and CRM tools, because in most cases the users are the very people who are best acquainted with business goals and what matters are fundamental to a competitive advantage.

These are only some of the general issues that characterize the automation status of non-structured management support systems.

Since the automation of enterprise activities began, it has seen three different and identifiable steps. The first phase was the automation of back office activities. This should lead to lower operational costs along with a higher level of efficiency. The second step was the automation of front office activities, together with the adaptation of first-generation DSSs. In this case, the aim was to improve effectiveness and to achieve the planned economic results. The last stage of development was the automation of non-structured decisional activities. The adaptation of such systems should allow attainment of a lasting competitive advantage over the competition and implementation of the enterprise's strategy.

While the first two steps are complete, most enterprises are currently dealing with the automation of non-structured decisional activities.

Many projects have been carried out, many other are now under way, and others will be planned in the immediate future. On the basis of experience in Italian and foreign companies, some consultants now propose best practices for the implementation of these systems. Other competitors have defined development methodologies. In general, all the operators contribute to the definition of standards aimed at the avoidance of failed Business Intelligence and CRM projects.

What are the fundamental issues to be evaluated in a Business Intelligence or a CRM project so as to obtain lasting economic advantages and valid support for the company's strategy?

According to the results of a research study conducted by CeTIF (Centro di Tecnologie Informatiche e Finanziarie), an academic research centre belonging to the Catholic University of the Sacred Heart in Milan, the most important issues that have to be considered are:

1. Identification and classification of business objectives,
2. Information quality,
3. Development methodologies and design, focused on users and based on the needs of the different business areas,
4. Identification of different user profiles,
5. Selection process for product choices,
6. Ways of disseminating information,
7. Technological architecture,
8. Organizational changes needed.

I.   Identification and Classification of Business Objectives

As in all technological projects, it is necessary to outline the business objectives that the users want to achieve. Moreover, one of the most important requirements for any Business Intelligence and CRM project is a profound knowledge of legacy systems, which helps in identification of the best architectural solution and indicates how to determine what kinds of data and information have to be fed into the new system.

At first glance, these can appear commonplace considerations, but such entities as the usage of operational data, the alignment time of Business Intelligence and CRM systems with the operational ones, the identification and integration with external information providers, data granularity and the temporal dimension of archiving depend on it. Furthermore, it is essential for it to become clear during the analysis phase that the development approach of a Business Intelligence and CRM project is profoundly different from that of an operational system.

Finally, it must also be pointed out that we seldom consider what data analysis models are used to implement archives of Business Intelligence and CRM solutions (information archive, datamart or data warehouse). This often limits the handling of data, which might be not usable for data mining systems. Data mining allows the generation of customer profiles and behaviours that can appropriately be fed into marketing campaign systems and all the other components of CRM.

II.   Information Quality

The data warehouse alone does not guarantee information quality. It is, however, a basic "introduction" to it.

Rigorous and systematic certification of data is becoming more and more important. Analytical databases that do not have any formal and systematic certification tend to lose value and usually cause problems when they need to be lined up with new business needs. Therefore, information quality becomes a strong driver for companies. It depends on: the business and the end-user's problems, the information need supporting the decision-making activities, the accuracy of the information (in the right place and time), and the consistency of information, which is obtained through:

- The creation of indicators, precalculated values, and interpretation of indicators,

- Alignment with new data/information,

- The updating schedule.

III.   Development Methodologies and Design Based on Users and on the Needs of the Different Business Areas

As already specified, it is important to consider all needs of the different business areas, and by adapting motivational means and coherent development approaches the users should become deeply involved in the project. In this way they become, so to speak, the real "owners" of the Business Intelligence and CRM solutions. Training workshops and task forces can help with understanding of the technological issues and in the implementation of stable and complete solutions.

The development process based on users consists of the eight activities shown in Figure I.

IV.   Identification of Different User Profiles

The identification of different user profiles implies that it is necessary to acquire a profound understanding of the needs of each user, their role in the company and their interaction with the system. In this context, homogeneous groups of users should be identified (principles of identification: information they look for, kind of activity, role, etc.).

Table I proposes a matrix that classifies different kinds of users with reference to a group of variables.

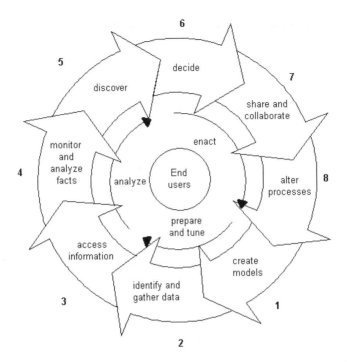

Figure I.   The development process of a Business Intelligence solution based on users (Source: Gartner Group)

Table I.   Classification of different kinds of users: the main variables to be considered

	Line managers	Knowledge workers	Senior management
Analysis complexity			
Strategic decision making			
Deepness of data			
Data usage capability			
Wideness of the available information base			
Tactical decision making			
Ease of usage			
Required personalization			

V. The Selection Process of Alternative Packages

After classifying the users, it is important to identify products and solutions that best fit in with the defined group of users and with the functionalities and interaction modes of the systems. The factors we have to consider in this case are the functionalities required of the different solutions (along with their characteristics: flexibility, scalability, etc.) and the modes of use in accordance with the different user categories.

Figure II illustrates a matrix based on two variables that explain how solutions for different categories of users can be developed.

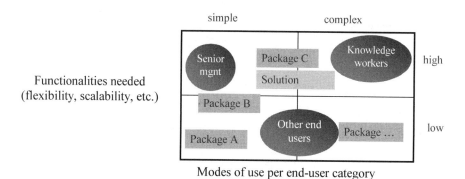

Functionalities needed
(flexibility, scalability, etc.)

Modes of use per end-user category

Figure II.   Selection of process solutions

VI. Ways of Providing Information

There are different ways of processing and disseminating information. These are basically identified by two criteria: kind of use and kind of support.

The main features of the first criterion are:

- User's mobility,
- Frequency of use,
- Degree of analysis complexity,
- Complexity of data,
- Available bandwidth,
- Frequency of data modification,
- Sharing level of applications,

- Scalability,
- Cost per user.

On the other hand, the main features of the second criterion concern the modes of interaction with the system and are related to the kind of support and the infrastructure adapted:

- Personal computer (or at least one not permanently connected to the Internet),
- Client/server (distributed),
- Internet-based technologies (intranet, extranet).

On the basis of the analyses carried out in this phase and their results, and with due consideration for the mode of use and the kind of support adapted, it is possible to identify how broad an application should be extended (Figure III).

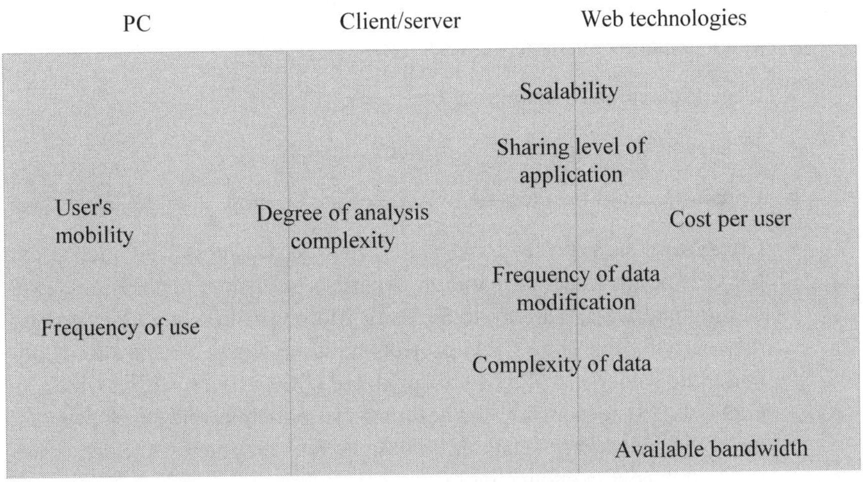

| PC | Client/server | Web technologies |

- Scalability
- Sharing level of application
- User's mobility
- Degree of analysis complexity
- Cost per user
- Frequency of data modification
- Frequency of use
- Complexity of data
- Available bandwidth

Figure III. Distributed application: users' support

VII. The Technological Architecture

The main aspects to be considered at the different levels of the technological architecture are:

1. The infrastructure,
   - Data storage and data management systems,
   - Connectivity,

2. The applications,

- Management system: user administration, security, data dictionary, and batch data processing,
- User level,
  - Data retrieval,
  - Visualization and exploration,
  - Calculators,
  - Publishing and distribution systems (or systems for the publication and distribution of information).

VIII. Organizational Change

The main organizational change necessitated by the introduction of business intelligence and CRM systems that support non-structured decisional activities are:

- Change management processes,
- Decentralization of activities,
- IT capability enhancement of business units,
- Enhancement of business knowledge of the IT shops at all levels,
- Creation of new professional skills, such as Business Intelligence and CRM expertise, data preparation expertise, statistical applications, Data Mining and Data Warehouse Systems. Moreover, in many cases companies carrying out large CRM projects build up a new organizational unit under the leadership of a newly appointed CRM officer, within which the CRM staff is responsible for defining the guidelines on developing and improving customer relations initiatives and programmes. Such a unit has both business and technological capabilities.

1 The Theoretical Framework of CRM

1.1 Environment and Technical Core

CRM projects are more and more destined to address two opposing concepts: efficiency and effectiveness. On the one hand a company needs to be effective on the market in order to manage relationships with customers, maintain its market share and improve its market penetration; on the other hand the company needs to be efficient. This means that IT departments need to conduct careful evaluations of IT investments and projects, as it is very difficult to understand whether initiatives have a return on investments or at least a direct and clear payback.

'Efficiency' and 'effectiveness' are undoubtedly misused, or at best overused, words. As a matter of fact, the creation of an organizational structure able to ensure both efficiency and effectiveness at the same time is the ultimate dream of everyone involved in company organization. Nevertheless, according to leading scholars, the roads that lead to efficiency can be, and in some cases even must be, different from those that lead to effectiveness. In other words, in short, efficiency requires a stable set-up, lots of routine, and a massive quantity of ex ante rules; on the other hand, to achieve effectiveness it is necessary to enhance personal initiative, motivation, ability to make decisions in ambivalent situations, and so on. This is why one of the basic problems in major companies is how to combine both roads successfully and make them coexist while refraining from low-quality compromises. Possible solutions come from Thompson (1967) and Lawrence and Lorsch (1967). The latter authors offer their own interpretation of the "segmented" organization, which is based on the well-known differentiation/integration logic: on the differentiation side, the point of having organizational units also specializing according to different efficiency/effectiveness targets emerges clearly, as shown in Fig. 1.1.

Equally well known, though less highly valued, are Thompson's *technical core* and *boundary-spanning components*. The first one is the company's "engine room", i.e., the area where product/service production takes place. Such an area needs to be protected and preserved from external influences, because it produces efficiency and therefore needs stability (Maggi, 1989; Decastri, 1984; Thompson, 1967).

Stability makes it possible to define and to operate on an organizational subsystem, which is *mechanical* in its nature (Burns and Stalker, 1961).

Boundary-spanning components, on the other hand, have a side-target: they are the technical core's protection system and their task is to attenuate or even to eliminate

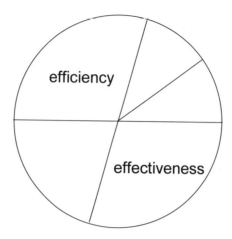

Figure 1.1   Efficiency and effectiveness

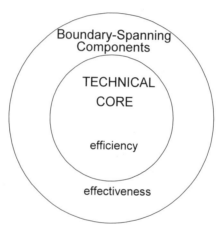

Figure 1.2   Boundary-spanning components and technical core

environment and market instability without giving up flexibility. They "translate" market expectations and transmit them to the "engine room." The company envisaged by Thompson has the configuration shown in Fig. 1.2.

In this second case, integration is no longer horizontal, but vertical. The issue is not how to coordinate different functions, but how to transmit the so-called customer's voice into the engine room, that is to say into the heart of the organizational system. It is a rather complex activity, which has always been one of organization's weakest points: we need only think about all the effort invested in sales and production programming tools, which have always yielded poor results.

Electronic technology seems capable of giving an important contribution in this field through enhanced and well-grounded knowledge of the market and of customers, who are a truly unpredictable species.

1.2   From Decision Support Systems to CRM: Main Steps in Evolution

The steps in the evolution of management information systems are the result of a large number of contributions, which through several decades have brought about progressive refinement of the methodological approach to systems management and the achievement of largely popular conceptual models, such as Management Information Systems, Decision Support Systems, and Executive Information Systems (Iivari, 1992).

A complete analysis of these approaches is not the issue here. Nevertheless, some of the main aspects must be called to mind, in order to allow us to spot the stages that have led to modern Customer Relationship Management (CRM) systems.

Management Information Systems were born to supply top management with the data necessary to control internal processes and plan resources correctly, as already mentioned by Anthony – who used to differentiate between operational and executive control – as long ago as in 1965 (Anthony, 1965).

The following contributions in the way of automated decision-help systems (Decision Support Systems) have their roots in two stimulating research trends: decision mechanism studies and interactive information systems. They were born to support decision-makers in the analysis of semistructured problems.

Last but not least came Executive Information Systems, which, according to Rockart's definition, were designed expressly to support summit power decisions (Rockart, 1988).

Looking back a few decades, we notice how all these approaches have found real applications in the complex mosaic we call a management information system. The most interesting results did not come at once, but only when the available technology allowed the realization of user-friendly systems. However, in many cases such systems proved not to be capable of satisfying company requirements fully so as to deliver relevant information in an integrated way.

Introduction of client/server architectures, improvement in database management techniques, and diffusion of high-performance workstations are just some of the factors that have allowed the spread of decision support forecast in Scott-Morton's studies in 1971, albeit with a 10-year delay. The consequences of technological innovation have gone further, however.

The last few year is characterized by the widespread acceptance of the Internet and of company intranets at every level. A common and easily operated access interface allows to data and information from different sources to be shared and used for different purposes (Lucas, 1992). Thanks to the new functionalities offered by the net, information flows will experience further development, which will be accompanied by increased organizational and economic relevance of information processing activities.

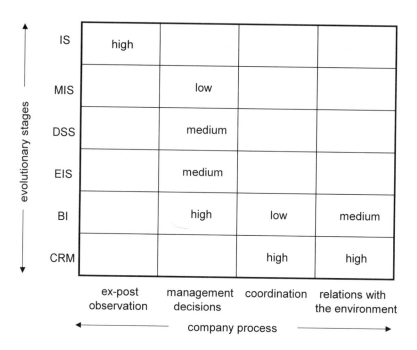

Table 1.1   Decision systems: evolutionary stages and company processes

Unfortunately, even though information technology is progressing rapidly, so far no technical tool or automation mechanism has proved able to translate the greater data availability into a significant improvement in company decision processes (Österle, 1995; Peppers, Rogers, Dorf, 1998).

As a complement to the growing diffusion of decision support-oriented systems, today's technology once more offers a wide range of options and solutions which enable the extension of decision activities in other company areas.

At first, technological innovation allowed the development of some decision supports, which were mostly not integrated into the existing information system. Data structures, data-saving approaches and operational system architecture were designed to provide exclusive support to administrative and accounting activities. Subsets were made from existing archives in order to create a new database which could, after proper "restructuring", be used to initiate management support applications (Berry, Linoff, 1997; Berry, Linoff, 1999; Ciborra, 1996).

This process caused great data alignment problems with the operational system and consequently jeopardized analysis reliability, and especially in those industries where management involved intensive use of information systems. Later on, at the end of the 1980s, new trends emerged in the direction of increasing integration of operational and analytical information systems, which set off the diffusion of so-called business intelligence systems. Such systems automate the decision process through systematic access to a database, which makes it possible to carry out analyses and extract information and thus to understand those phenomena that lead to an improvement of the decision process or at least reduce the uncertainties of the decisions to be taken. Some members of the business intelligence family are decision support systems, executive information systems, and all tools that enable querying and reporting activities (Imhoff, Loftis, Geiger, 2001). Reference technological architecture also shows a greater integration between operational and decision support systems (Inmon, 1996). The consequent popularity of data warehouse and data mining systems is now pushing toward ever-increasing integration, which in turn leads to increasing automation in some of the decision activities (Kelly, 1997).

Progressive consolidation of integrated architectures (the operational part with the analytical part) allows all decision activities to be finalized per company area (Ciborra, 2000).

In particular, and owing to the creation of datamarts, they give users and managers access to all the data and appropriate information that can be found in a company's information system, and they even integrate external sources, which enrich the archive content used to "feed" the decision process. This is how dedicated datamarts come to life: one each for management control, synthesis systems, marketing, internal auditing, etc. (see Fig. 1.3). With the aid of data analysis systems (data mining systems in particular) they can uncover hidden patterns, thus helping those concerned to spot interesting points and providing for directions that are likely to reduce the degree of uncertainty in future decisions (Kimball, 1996; Poe, 1996).

This context of the aim of this present work calls for a close examination of the main aspects concerned with management, organization, and automation of company-to-customer relationships.

On the one hand, marketing information systems have gained advantages by the introduction of business intelligence technologies, namely data warehouses and data mining. On the other hand, several factors have led to reconsideration of their strategic value and matters such as the progressive evolution of the Internet, the increased competition level, and the ability to operate in geographically distant markets through e-business initiatives. Therefore, integrated solutions that are well-suited to allowing for automation of company-customer interaction are being looked for, in order to gain a durable competitive advantage (Porter, Millar, 1985).

1.3   Research Objectives and Purpose of Present Work

What follows is an attempt at a research path which aims to define what is happening in the field and to start a theoretical reading of it.

As the first aspect, it has to be noted that CRM phenomena can be studied from a number of different perspectives and reality aggregation levels. Such alternatives gravitate into each discipline field. This work is an investigation trying to conciliate Thompson's theoretical reflections on organizational and information systems

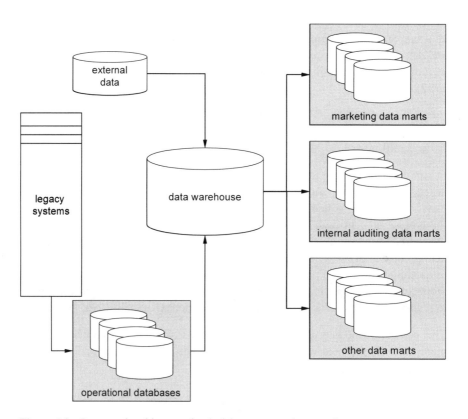

Figure 1.3   Integrated architecture for decision support: data warehouse

studies concerning, in particular, information technology for CRM in the banking industry. The research object may therefore be split into two parts: first, definition of the phenomena at issue; second, implications of organization and change management, brought about by the introduction of the said systems in the banking industry, in view of Thompson's theoretical approach.

In short, the purpose is to check whether, as Thompson suggests, it is possible to isolate a bank's "technical core" from environmental influences through the creation of "units in contact with the outside" that are able to "mitigate or level environment fluctuations" and to promote "adaptation to restraints-contingent factors not controlled by the bank." Are these banks capable of responding flexibly to the present profound technological changes, meaning CRM systems in particular, and to the increased environmental complexity?

In this connection, the research is based on the analysis of important banking CRM experiences, and its aims are to seek and define reference technologies and to analyse customer relationship management variations seen in its three main domains: business processes, technological subsystem, and customer life cycle.

The approach in this first phase is qualitative/methodological in nature, aimed at verifying the qualitative conditions (such as impact of marketing and information systems on organization, adjustment of competencies, critical points emerging during the creation of CRM systems, integration between information systems, and evaluation of the ability to achieve business goals consistently with the technology adapted). The empirical verification of possible solutions is based on the Italian banks that are presently creating their own CRM systems: a review of the phenomena is presented on the basis of Thompson's approach.

2 CRM Project Organization in the Financial Industry

2.1 Basic Motivations for CRM

Evolving technology and the constant changes affecting the banking industry are increasingly pushing toward research into integrated solutions, in order to maintain and enhance customer relationship. It is not only about seeking technically updated solutions: the practical issue is how to intervene in the bank's business processes so as to turn banks into customer-centred organizations (Brown, 1999).

In the past, banks invested a lot in developing and maintaining operational systems. In the last few years they have allocated increasing proportions of their budgets to the implementation of applications for marketing decision support. Most of these have been "offline" initiatives aimed at improving the information base and finding the best possible way of using the existing huge databases (Belking, Croft 1992). That is to say that there have never been any major systematic information restructuring projects, much less data warehouse or datamart projects, that would have made it possible to use modern decision support systems (Brown, 2000; Chablo, 1999).

Such initiatives, as of today, can hence be considered as the umpteenth (stratified) layer of the information system. As previously mentioned, a bank's information system is made up of a number of subsystems and application layers, developed time after time from different databases, which are not integrated or have proved hard to integrate. In fact, "layering" itself is responsible for the current inability to exploit databases fully and thus better support decision-making (Rockart, 1979; Willcocks, Feeny, Islei, 1997).

Moreover, there are a number of factors leading banks to reconsider their own marketing strategies in search of a lasting competitive advantage (Porter, Millar, 1985). Some of these factors are increasingly pressing competition, which is due partly to new competitors entering the market, greater size of banks owing to continuous merger and acquisition operations, with a consequent increase in the number of customers that need to be dealt with, and, last but not least, the escalating acceptance of the Internet and e-business.

The banks have reacted promptly to this new scenario: there are significant cases of banks, not just in Italy, that through the definition of new, multichannel-oriented strategies have reinforced their position, conquering sizeable shares of the market. By adapting adequate strategies, they have been able to hit the market successfully, creating considerable value and state-of-the-art technology, and exploiting the competitive advantage originating from the new channels (Scott Tillet, 2000; Carignani, 2001).

However, today, some years after the explosion of these new channels, things seem to be back to square one. Almost every bank equipped itself with the said new distribution channels, which are used to maintain relationships with existing customers. In keeping with banking industry traditions, within just a few months the product/service innovations seemed never to have taken place.

Nowadays, owing to the new channels, banks are able to offer products and services at average costs that are significantly lower than traditional ones. Channel multiplication, however, does not ensure enhanced profitability (Hall, 2001). From an organizational point of view, the increase in the number of contact points implies an increased coordination of all initiatives aimed at maintaining and developing customer relationship (Bach, 2001; Gostick, 2000).

As mentioned above, while initially the use of the new channels was seen as a possible way of maintaining a continuous relationship with the customer by offering products and services, basic conditions have now changed, and they allow better exploitation of the channels themselves. Through new approaches and use of the available technology it is now possible to understand the actual needs of customers, so as to operate on an ad hoc basis and offer services to each customer segment through the most suitable channel (branch, ATM, mailing, e-mail, financial promoters, remote banking with customised browser interface, telephone banking, interactive TV, etc.).

Customer approach is now completely different, and new solutions are required to manage and organize customer relationships (Peppers, Rogers, 1997).

Besides traditional branches and ATM or POS, customers can now use "new" channels, such as home banking, trading on line, telephone banking, and interactive TV. The sales network, too, appears to be more effective, since financial promoters using a remote connection are now potentially able to create the best possible product or service for each type of customer.

Today's technology allows easy replication of products. This, however, will provide a push towards mass personalization, with creation of tailored products per customer profile at the most appropriate time and through the proper channel. In its turn, the offer of customized products and services which satisfy all customers' needs requires a thorough redefinition of sales processes (Brown, 2000; Österle 1995). The ability to intervene effectively by way of internal organizational variables is one of the critical factors in the success of CRM projects. This requires the transition from a product-oriented to a customer-oriented business process (Lee, 2000)

2.2   CRM Drivers and Key Factors

A number of factors have contributed to the growing relevance of CRM as a source of competitive advantage. They can be subdivided into four classes (Hamil, 2000):

1. Market drivers,
2. Customer-related drivers,
3. Business drivers,
4. Technological drivers.

An evaluation of impact by way of company can be made for each of the above classes (Table 2.1).

In the past, a few companies have begun CRM projects, just developing systems based on new technologies and neither identifying an appropriate strategy able to support the business goals nor focusing on change management initiatives able to support the radical modifications of the processes involved (Burn, 1989).

The creation of a customer relationship strategy is the very first step in a CRM project. It requires various steps:

1. *Knowledge:* It is necessary to identify the most profitable customers.
2. *Listening:* The emphasis is on customer loyalty; therefore it is imperative to find out key values and needs for each customer class.
3. *Growth:* Through communication and value production in the most suitable way for each customer class, the company is able to develop a relationship with its customers.
4. *Results evaluation.*

Again, to face these stages properly, the company has to review and integrate its infrastructures and business processes, paying particular attention to two crucial factors: communication and knowledge sharing.

As for communication (PricewaterhouseCoopers, 2000), four main classes can be identified:

- *Mass communication*: It has a great impact, though it is generally not aimed at a particular market, and it is brought about through media and traditional channel advertising.

- *Communication per market segment*: The company seeks the optimum combination of channel and their relative frequency of use, so as to reach specific segments.

- *Direct marketing*: aimed at a particular portion of a specific market segment, using tools such as mail, e-mail, telephone.

- *One-to-one communication:* based on direct interaction between company and customer, via e-mail, telephone, mail or sales agents. It is usually supported by CRM systems.

Table 2.1   CRM drivers and impacts

Market drivers	Impacts
Competitive environment, standardization of products and services, reduced switching costs, aggressive price competition, and saturation/maturity of markets	An effective CRM strategy is nowadays a critical factor in achieving objectives such as differentiation and customer loyalty
Customer drivers	**Impacts**
End of mass marketing, growing importance of one-to-one relationships	As a consequence of the end of mass marketing, today "the customer is king": customers have access to a wide range of personalized products and services, can better evaluate purchase convenience, and can demand high-level post-sales assistance. In short, the traditional four P's of the marketing mix have been replaced by the four C's of rational marketing: Costs, Convenience, Communication, and Customer needs and wants
Business drivers	**Impacts**
80/20 rule (80% of profits are produced by 20% of customers); acquiring new customers is much more expensive than maintaining existing ones; "loyal" customers are more profitable than new ones; a longer customer relationship brings higher profits	Production of added value for customers is the real source of a company's competitive advantage
Technology drivers	**Impacts**
Development of interactive communication tools such as call centres, development of front office solutions, of data mining, etc.	IT and Internet allow the use of new channels to enhance the retention rate of profitable customers while reducing the service costs of the less profitable ones

Communication has a fundamental role, as the level of company-to-customer dialogue shows the degree of CRM strategy development reached by the company (Fig. 2.1).

For instance, if a company entertains a superficial relationship with its customers, the relationship will be concerned merely with product-based aspects (such as features, price). If, on the contrary, the company implements a fully customer-oriented strategy, it will be able to develop a deep and lasting relationship. The

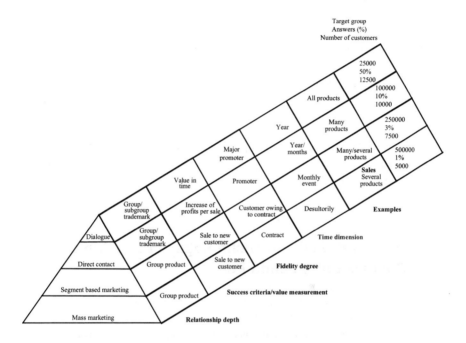

Figure 2.1 CRM development stages and different communication forms (Pricewater-houseCoopers Consulting, 2000)

depth of the relationship, customer value in time and the investment in maintenance of the relationship become critical success factors (Shesbunoff, 1999; Scott Tillet, 2000).

Another important issue is customer knowledge sharing (Keene, 2001).

The company has to develop systems that enable it to:

- Gather information on customers,
- Organize data so as to perform effective analyses,

- Use the customer knowledge gathered to implement value-creating initiatives,

- Share knowledge with the customer and within the company.

Since good customers are a *scarce resource,* it is important for the company to manage all contact points effectively, to gather all necessary information, and to attain ideal customer knowledge. It must be borne in mind that each contact or communication has to be regarded as positive from the customer's point of view. Every new datum or piece of information about the customer has to be carefully saved and processed to improve the company's corporate knowledge.

All the information gathered must then be made available to all the company employees, so that everyone can have a full understanding of the customer's characteristics and thus be able to offer a customized service answering specific needs. The value of knowledge can be measured as the difference between the cost of acquiring a new customer and the cost of maintaining an existing customer. A fundamental issue for the company is to be able to increase the value of the customer and possibly reduce customer loss *(churn rate).* All this becomes possible only when a CRM programme is made up of strategies, CRM information systems, and process re-engineering (Egan, 1999; Eager, 2001; Angel, 2000; Bielski, 2000).

2.3   Organizational and Technological Evolution of Customer Interaction Points

In the last few years, customer contact points (branches, call centres and financial promoters) have been completely rethought. This is particularly evident if we consider the organizational interventions of recent years, which have noticeably strengthened the sales and market relationship structures. Just think of "branches", which have turned into "financial shops", and ATMs, which are no longer simple holes in the wall but have been converted into multiservice terminals. Today's banking operations are different, and customer contact provides the most suitable opportunity for cross-selling or up-selling initiatives. However, physical restructuring has only occasionally been accompanied by interventions on organizational mechanisms (Blattberg, Getz, Thomas, 2001). In other words, integration of information infrastructures and revision of organizational criteria are yet to come, and the frequently cited "customer-centric" organization seems to be even further away (Bielski, 2001).

This last aspect, according to which the customer is placed in the middle of the value chain, should lead banks towards a new dimension, where the approach to the customer is completely overturned (Decastri, De Marco, Rajola, 2001). The transition is from marketing actions trying to associate product classes with customer clusters, to actions able to provide ad hoc products and services through better comprehension of customer attitudes and behaviour (Burnett, 2000).

The goals of in-depth understanding of customers' purchase preferences and the ability to anticipate their needs seem to be within reach. In fact, banks have an information base potentially available to them that remains mostly unused: transactions carried out (Hall, 1999). Every time the customer is in touch with his bank, he implicitly provides information on his characteristics, needs and preferences. Transactions carried out are powerful data and information, which, used properly, allow elaboration of the individual customer's purchase profile and determination of the interaction channel that suits him best, and outline his life cycle in such a way that the bank can understand how the relationship evolves over time (Hall, 1999; Gilmore, Pine, 2000).

These are just a few of the motivations that explain the investment to be made in CRM projects over the next few years.[1]

CRM aims to make the relationship between bank and customer as profitable as possible. This helps the bank to figure out which are the best customers, the ones it cannot afford to lose, those who are bound to grow, and those who will turn out to be bad payers. The same goes for an individual customer's needs, the services he requires and the channels that provide them and the offers he might be interested in. It is all about anticipating and guiding requirements through the creation of new customer-oriented products and services (Bennet, 2002; Morris, 2002).

Banks' attitudes and choices up to now have revealed definite difficulty in locating effective approaches and modes of operation. Environment limitations represent the limits that are liable to jeopardize the project's success in terms of lack of an effective change management programme.

2.4   CRM in the Banking Industry

Well-known studies performed at international level have pointed out that 65% of the profits are supplied by a mere 20% of the company's customers, another 25% of the profits being owed to another 20% of the customers, whereas the remaining 60% of customers together account for only the remaining 10% (Brown, 2000). In the financial industry, the balance is even worse; in some cases a small percentage

---

[1] According to a research performed in Europe by META Group (2000) the average investment for a CRM project amounts to 2.5 mill. Euro. Other research studies, always by META Group, foresee an average of 3.5/4 million Euro altogether for the banking sector.

of customers can even yield negative profitability (Free, Close, Eisenfeld, De Lotto, 2001). We might add that acquisition costs for a new customer are up to five times as high as the maintenance costs for an existing one (Burnett, 2000).[2]

2.5   Definition and Purposes of CRM

Although the expression CRM did not begin to spread until the late 1990s, it actually refers to well-known and, in some cases, thoroughly studied concepts. Many CRM components have already been created and are currently being used by companies; we need only think of one-to-one marketing systems (Peppers, Rogers, Dorf, 1998), sales strength automation systems (Petersen, 1997) and customer relationship personalization systems (Kotler, 1999). The main difference is that the past approach favoured "automation islands", so that initiatives were not aimed at full integration and redefinition of organizational approaches. These off-line applications allowed partial and nonrepeatable goals.

In contrast, the success of new technologies and the rethinking of organizational approaches now enables progressive integration with legacy systems. Such organizational and technological integration makes it easier for the bank to achieve its business objectives. It is perhaps the first time that strategy, organization and information technologies are marching side by side to achieve a highly desired alignment (Earl, 1989; McKeen, Smith, 1996). What is more, project managers seem to have realized that organization is the fundamental ingredient in CRM initiatives.

There are a number of definitions of CRM. This depends partly on the different solutions offered by software vendors or system integrators. Each provider associates only particular aspects of CRM with his product range and with the technologies it employs. On the other hand, no systematic academic study has yet mastered CRM issues that offer a complete definition. Further, considering companies' perception (and, more to the point, banks' perceptions) of what CRM is in terms of definition, subsystems and achievable targets, it is plain that a proper systematization of the concepts involved is still a long way off. This is even more true if the analysis is focused on the banking industry and on the relationship between the evolution of CRM systems technology and organizational studies (Decastri, De Marco, Rajola, 2001).

Owing to these difficulties and to the lack of a unanimous definition, an attempt at this will be made here; it does not pretend to be exhaustive, but will merely offer a broad outline of the various sections of CRM's and its objectives.

---

[2] However, the presence of supposedly all-but-profitable customers allows sharing fixed costs, thus enhancing the profitability of the better customers.

CRM is a business strategy aiming to understand and to anticipate the needs of existing customers and to seek new ones who might potentially be interested in products or services offered by the bank.

Therefore, CRM may be regarded as a set of technological and organizational mechanisms intended to buffer market instability through better knowledge of environmental variables, particularly market variables, in order to anticipate customers' needs, rendering production activities more stable and programmable. To achieve such goals it is necessary to design new processes and to create systems based on state-of-the-art, integrated, technologies, so as to give new and consistent support to customer interaction through all the bank's communication channels (Brown, 2000).

CRM projects last several years and can be divided into a number of separate yet coordinated initiatives, based on a consistent design concerning customer-centred processes, communication channels, and all the company's organizational units. From a technological point of view, CRM requires identification of the operational archives containing customer data (register, carried-out transactions, products owned, sector of activity, etc.), consolidation and integration of this with external information sources through creation of a new "centralized archive." This helps to simplify the analysis activities; to make sophisticated analysis tools available, and to seek customer models and behaviour rules; analysis results are distributed throughout the company and to all customer interaction systems (physical channels, financial promoters, virtual channels, call centres, direct marketing systems, etc.). The process ends with the updating of the legacy system archives after actions have been carried out and according to changes in the customer's profile (Decastri, De Marco, Rajola, 2001).

Achievement of CRM goals thus requires an integrated approach, so as to single out and manage each customer's life cycle, with due consideration for all interaction points with the company. It is thus necessary to coordinate all actions aimed at: seeking a new customer or attracting the attention of an existing one, where a new product or service is concerned; and enhancing negotiation, transaction, and relationship management support activities (McKenna, 1993).

Hence, CRM must be seen as a business system, or a systematic approach to customer's life cycle management which associates the most suitable technologies with business requirements. Integrated customer life cycle management calls for convergence of three separate domains: sales process, CRM information system, and life cycle understanding for each customer cluster. At the front end this enables the customer, according to his specific needs, to choose his interaction channel, the product/service he is interested in, and whether to carry out the transaction (be it a provision or a mere item of information). At the back end, the transaction carried out updates the systems (operational and analytical) and activates supply chain and service delivery processes.

In short, CRM can be regarded as a business system or a systematic approach to customer life cycle management, which aligns processes and technology.

The architecture of CRM systems requires the use of technology to automate front-end processes (sales, support services, marketing, distribution channels, etc.) and integrate them into operational systems and to feed information to the data warehouse and data marts; finally, it allows reuse of information for data analysis activities that can be exploited by marketing automation and marketing campaign systems.

2.6   The CRM Ecosystem

The CRM ecosystem is made up of three fundamental components:

- Analytical CRM,
- Operational CRM,
- Collaborative CRM.

The three components singled out in the previous figure are the "fields of action" of CRM; they are closely linked to one another, because the lack or inadequacy of any one dimension jeopardizes the functioning of the entire system (Ptacek, 2000).

2.6.1   The Analytical Component

The company's data and information on customers are analysed, the objective being management and enhancement of business performances (Dyché, 2000). To this end, CRM solutions use an informational platform featuring centralized archives, into which customer-level data flow, fed by operational systems' databases. In the analytical component, data warehouse and the datamarts (on customers, products, campaigns, etc.) play the main part. In the information dimension, data are turned into systematized information leading to a better comprehension of business events (Kelly, 1997; Kimball, 1996; McKenna, 1993; Morse, Isaac, 1998; Peppers, Rogers, 1997). Using business intelligence tools in data analysis, for instance, we are able to divide the customers into homogeneous groups, building up profiles and creating behaviour models through evaluation of a number of parameters, such as loyalty, profitability, solvency and, last but not least, sensitivity to

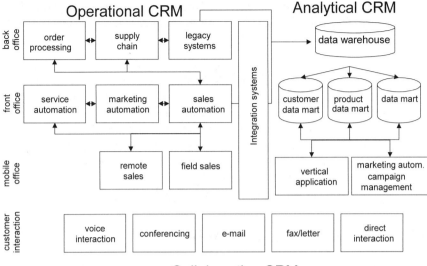

Figure 2.2   Source: adapted by META Group, 2000

particular marketing actions, which can therefore be effectively planned and moni-tored (Lee, 2000; Kotler, 1999; Groth, 1998; Brown, 2000).

The following list contains the main elements (shown in Fig. 2.2) of what is nor-mally known as analytical CRM. The fundamental subsystems of the analytical component are:

1. *Data warehouse (DWH):* This is a collection of *integrated, subject-oriented, time-variant* and *non-volatile* data supporting decision processes (Inmon, 1996). DWH data integration is a necessary condition for an ef-fective design, and it is what sets a DWH apart from every other decision support system (Kimball, 1996; Tulley, 2001).

2. *Datamarts:* These are smaller archives fed by the DWH and suitably de-signed to face particular business problems (Simon, 1998). CRM applica-tions mainly use the customer and service/product datamarts. Other data-marts can be developed if particular analyses need to be carried out.

3. *Other vertical applications:* Reporting systems and other systems aimed at monitoring particular situations connected with the bank's business, e.g. data mining systems and OLAP (online analytical process) belong to this category. Such systems can be used to uncover hidden relationships between data. Data mining, for instance, allows better understanding of

customer needs and combination of the most appropriate products and delivery channels for each client. An in-depth description of these systems is given in the following chapters.

4. *Marketing automation and campaign manager systems:* These are products designed to plan and monitor a marketing campaign. They are used to identify the product to be sold, any possible association with another product, the potentially interested customer class, and how the latter is to be contacted. The campaign will then be carried out in the system's transactional and collaboration components. Once the campaign has been carried out, the results of it are fed into the campaign management system (through the update of the marketing datamarts), so as to keep a record of all events relating to past actions (Eager, 2001).

2.6.2   The Operational Component

Business decisions taken in the analytical context are then carried out in the operational dimension, where operations take place. CRM operational technologies include "customer interaction" applications, integrated within front, back and mobile office. It offers a number of different utilities, such as: anagraphical data of each customer, highlighting of his attitudes and preferences, information on operations carried out (operational or inquiries, such as acquisitions or transfers) per channel, operational management of inbound and outbound marketing campaigns, and acquisition of an updated profile for each customer.

The operational CRM also supports back office activities (order management, supply chain and transactions with the bank's information system), front office activities (service automation, marketing automation, sales force automation) and mobile office activities concerning branch personnel, financial promoters and all other sales support services.

2.6.3   The Collaborative Component

Collaborative CRM allows for simplification of customer–bank contacts through definition of the most suitable channels and products/services for each individual customer (Carignani, 2001).

All marketing initiatives, which were formerly carried out directly in the branches, now require thorough revisiting of the customer management process. In the very recent past branches just allowed transactions to be carried out. Branch clerks did not have the cultural attitudes and capabilities to allow them to deal with customers in the sense of initiating proactive marketing actions or engaging in relationship management.

Currently available information tools, owing to the integration of analytical and operational CRM, permit quick spotting of customer classes interested in particular products/services and management of the offering options for these through all the existing channels (Gostick, 2000; Hamblen, 2000; Tynan, 2000). Clerks in the branches now have access to a set of front office tools which suggest to them both what kind of services they should push to each customer and an in-depth description of the characteristics of the product.

Therefore, banks can count on the same customer profile throughout all contact channels, and above all, customers have access to the entire service range from any channel, so that they can choose the most suitable contact point through a personalised interface (Tynan, 2000).

What is more, there is an increasing spread of signalling services concerning significant financial events from both the customer's and the bank's point of view: i.e. *push technology*-based systems. In the banking industry the most popular ones are: notification of daily variation of portfolio value; alerts for particular events, such as variation in discount rate or stock value rise beyond a particular range set by the customer; and notification to the customer that his bank account has gone into the red or has exceeded a given value. For instance, such surplus liquidity may be invested in financial tools provided by the bank, in order to enhance both the bank's and the customer's profitability (Puccinelli, 1999; Kiesnoski, 1999).

The main components of analytical CRM are all customer contact channels; an informational environment manages each interaction point (catalogued in the operational dimension) (Puccinelli, 1999).

2.7   The Organizational Perspective of CRM

As just shown, a complete CRM solution includes a number of hardware elements and software applications. Unfortunately, these alone are not able to guarantee the expected return on investments (Eilon, 2001). There is an aspect that is often neglected by companies, though it is fundamental in the creation and affirmation of a CRM system: this is the organizational component (Schneider, 2001). Not uncommonly, it represents the most critical issue for a successful CRM project.

Too often, the effects of technological innovation and introduction of new systems are neutralized by the lack of change management initiatives. In fact, from the writer's point of view, CRM is mainly an organizational initiative, which should, on the one hand, consider the environmental peculiarities the system has to face and, on the other, provide for a complete review of organizational variables and the selling processes (Mayes, 2001). Consequent structural changes require strong support from the bank's management, aiming to optimize change-related actions and sustain them over time, so as to allow for a progressive acceptance of the new modus operandi and minimization of resistance to the changes (Keenan, 2001; Keene, 2001).

The deep "organizational gap" caused by the introduction of CRM, if not properly supported by relevant change management interventions, could potentially neutralize the system's efficiency or, worse, irreversibly jeopardize the relationship with not-yet-loyal customers (Rigby, Reichheld, Schefter, 2002).

Hence, we need a definition including the organizational component as well: "CRM is a combination of organizational and technological mechanisms aiming to buffer market instability through better knowledge of environmental variables, particularly market variables, in order to anticipate customers' needs and make production activities more stable and programmable" (Decastri, De Marco, Rajola, 2001; Thompson, 1967).

Having said this, it is plain that the bank, while implementing the CRM solution, needs to be provided with adequate professional figures for it to derive full benefit from the innovations. This is why organizational interventions and revision of internal processes are at the roots of the ability to achieve CRM objectives. The issue is a better management of the customer's life cycle and definition of the steps necessary to attain a customer-centric organization.

In this way CRM can be considered an "organizational buffer" (Thompson, 1967) able to preserve the efficiency of the technical core through elimination of the instabilities typical of the banking market and environment, without giving up the flexibility the operational environment requires.

2.8   Data Analysis Techniques

We will now focus on CRM's analytical component, particularly on analysis techniques, by exploring one of CRM's main issues and trying to put it in context with the banking industry[3] (Berry, Linoff, 1997).

There are two distinct approaches to data analysis:

- *User driven:* The user interacts with the system through simple queries, ad hoc queries, and *OLAP* tools to create reports on business trends and customers' data. At the basis of this approach, there are "strong" or "moderate" hypotheses. Response time is generally quite short. Analysis complexity level is consistently low to medium.

---

[3] For a deeper knowledge of the other systems of the analytical component see the chapters below.

- *Data driven:* The system processes queries automatically or semi-automatically in order to generate statistic analyses, create behavioural models, and segment or find a priori unknown relationships. At the basis of this approach there are "light" hypotheses or none at all. The response time is long. The complexity level is high (Groth, 1998).

At company level, it is possible to single out three types of decisions: structured, semi-structured and unstructured (Anthony, 1965). What follows are the data analysis techniques suitable to assist the decisional process concerning unstructured decisions. Analyses carried out at strategic level to support the decision process may be classified as follows:

1. Standard query,

2. Multidimensional analyses,

3. Statistical analyses,

4. Data mining.[4]

2.8.1   Standard Query

These are the simplest methods available to the user for interrogation of the system. A query is a request for information directed to a database. The typical output is a report. Standard queries are defined during the creation of the system: therefore, they do not have to be rewritten every time. An example of query could be:

Show the list of all loans granted in January 2001.

The hypothesis at the base of the standard query is of the strong type: in other words, the customer is aware of a particular business phenomenon and wishes to have more information about it. The approach is therefore user driven. The complexity is low, and response time is short.

2.8.2   Multidimensional Analysis

Multidimensional analysis, that is to say ad hoc queries and OLAP analysis, is the next level. It allows the user to obtain more detailed information than is supplied in response to standard queries. A greater number of perspectives for data monitoring is provided. The typical output is again a report. An example could be the following:

---

[4] Referred to in later chapters.

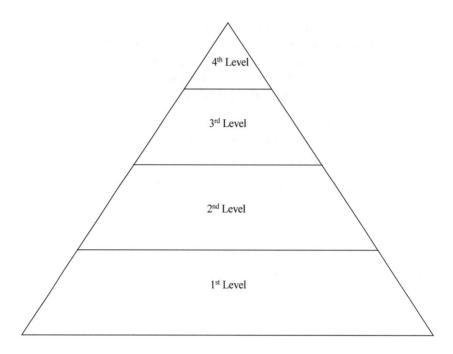

Figure 2.3   Decisional pyramid and data analysis levels

Visualize the list of all loans granted in January 2002 by each branch.

The hypothesis at the basis of a multidimensional analysis is a moderate one: the user wishes to deepen his knowledge of phenomena he is already familiar with. The approach, as in the standard query, is user driven. The complexity is medium to low, and the response time is generally short.

The analyses that are currently most popular are known as OLAP. They are performed using ad hoc systems, through which the user checks the data from the database (Delmater, Hancok, 2001).

Data are shown as an *n*-dimensional cube (hypercube), from which the information desired is extracted. OLAP's main feature is the ability to reach the desired information through subsequent approximations, with no need to express accurate hypotheses a priori.

The cube or, generally speaking, the multidimensional scheme, allows the user to consult the data from different perspectives at the same time, without having to specify the angle or the exact level of detail in advance. The data can then be aggregated or separated at any level. Using given variables for dimensions (cube edges) and aggregations it is possible to obtain very quick responses measurable in seconds.

There are two main classes of OLAP systems: ROLAP and MOLAP (plus some hybrid techniques such as HOLAP, which stands for hybrid OLAP, and DOLAP, meaning Desktop OLAP). ROLAP (Relational OLAP) refers to analyses on data contained in a relational database. If, on the other hand, data come from a multidimensional database the analyses are called MOLAP (Multidimensional OLAP). Relational databases are characterized by their simplicity of implementation, and multidimensional ones by promptness in responding to queries (Hall, 1999).

OLAP data analysis techniques are called *drill* and *slice and dice*. Using the first, it is possible either to go deep into the data (drill-down) or to climb the data hierarchy to enjoy an overall view (drill-up). The second and third allow the user to "rotate" the multidimensional cube in order to highlight the desired dimension with its data.

2.8.3 Statistical Analysis

Statistical analyses allow for greater depth in data investigation than can be achieved through standard query or multidimensional analysis. A bank can use them to evaluate average customer value, specifically by forecasting customer loss or relationship duration and classifying customers according to qualitative and quantitative variables. This enables bank staff, for instance, to comprehend how to interact with a given customer segment.

The hypothesis at the basis of statistical analyses is a light one, for the user is not in a position to foresee the composition of the analysis output. The approach is data driven, as opposed to the two previous cases. Analysis complexity is medium to high, and the response time might be long. The analysis is carried out using the appropriate statistical tools.

2.9   The Main Requirements for a CRM Solution

As previously mentioned, CRM initiatives have to be seen as system integration projects. As a matter of fact, the market does not seem to provide products or product suites that are able to cover all CRM areas. Software vendors' offers, though they might seem to be integrated, do not in the majority of cases appear to fulfil all necessary requirements for a complete customer relationship management solution. It is thus sensible to highlight the main functional and technological requirements of a CRM solution. The aim is to point out how a complete solution, integrated into the information system, is much more than the choice of a product. It is understandable, then, that the analysis and mastering of each of the following points constitutes a network of operations to be carried out in a coordinated fashion (Young, 2002). The point is that a CRM project usually lasts more than 2 years and each initiative can be split into a number of coordinated subprojects, in order to automate the customer relationship, integrate the existing systems, and support all the actions required to implement the system itself (Rajola, 2000). Hence the importance, as already mentioned, of interventions concerning process review and design, change management, evaluation of business and technology gaps at all levels, and training of end-users in the operation of systems, such as those with which they have never had the chance to interact before. We need only consider that some branch operators who have been using operational systems for years will be asked to turn into skilful vendors. They will be provided with a system using approaches completely separate from that of conventional operational systems. In CRM interaction matters, the ability to access relevant information at any given moment and the possibility of gathering the results of initiatives undertaken are just some of the features that allow the bank to improve constantly on the knowledge of its customers and the quality of its information bases.

All functional and technological requirements, as well as all main features of a complete CRM system (Rajola, 2000), are listed below.

2.9.1   Main Functional Requirements

1. Scalability of the solution,

2. Orientation, adaptation, and personalization according to business goals,

3. Vast and flexible database (conceptual data model, creation of a logical/physical model, ability to extend and add fields),

4. Flexibility in development of vertical applications,

5. Simplicity in management and administration,

6. Pragmatism in creation (gradual growth, open development, maximum personalization, change flexibility, etc.),

7. Easy operation (standard Windows, Help, Wizard utilities),

8. Schooling and training,

9. Change management interventions.

2.9.2   Main Technological Requirements

1. Quick development (RAD – rapid application development),

2. Database support (complete reliability on supported database),

3. Data synchronization (simultaneous support of multiple data synchronizations through the LAN or WAN itself, or through combinations of LAN and remote users),

4. Business intelligence systems (data mining, data warehouse, etc.),

5. Sharing of information,

6. User interface (management and rendering of data through drop lists, panels, etc.),

7. Real-time integration with other applications (MS office, etc.),

8. Multichannel management (web access, call centre, e-mail, etc.),

9. Standard application developments (Windows interface, WEB, etc.),

10. Portability of system development and communication platform,

11. Integration with security systems.

2.9.3   Main Features and Requirements of a CRM System

1. "Anagraphic" management of the customer (the initial customer database must evolve toward a complete register bank stage).

2. Visualization/segmentation of customers by

   - Customer type (potential, acquired, promoter, acquaintance, "bringer", consultant, etc.),
   - Geographical area,
   - Switch with contacts.

3. Contact management,

   - Contact graphic network (tree structure, who has been brought, introduced, etc.),
   - Meeting memorandum and customer visits management (customer visit, visit in lounge, etc.),
   - List of contacts with customer (visits, phone calls, mail, e-mail, etc.).

4. Plan and schedule management,

   - Done and to do lists,
   - Schedules, e.g. for customer type, activity, geographical area.

5. Sales network management,

   - Proprietary network (promoter list, geographical area, profitability, etc.),
   - Deals and partnerships (list, geographical area, etc.).

6. Events and campaign management,

- Selection of a class of customers and association of this class with a campaign/event,
- Definition of follow-ups for each campaign,
- Feedback and campaign results,
- Tracking of activities.

7. Data importing,

- Selection of multimedia contacts (e.g. from Internet),
- Loading into the CRM system for assignment of campaigns or activities.

8. Reporting,

- Printout of customer data (complete but synthetic),
- Printout of campaigns and events,
- Printout of schedules (by period, activity, etc.),
- Statistics, analyses, graphs and simulations.

9. Research and selection,

- Visualization of customer register,
- Selection and visualization of information from different "views" (customer type, geographical area, associated promoter, customer introducer, acquirer, etc.),
- Creation of personalized views (templates).

10. Security,

- Different access levels (via password),
- Certification and authorization system.

11. Connections,

- External connection for promoters (on Internet),
- Remote data consulting (on Internet),
- Remote data updating (on Internet).

12. Interface with other applications,

- E-mail system (automatically sends e-mails),
- Fax system (automatically sends faxes),
- Office automation (generation of addresses for letters, label printing, etc.),
- Analytical tools (data mining, statistics, etc.).

2.10 A Study on CRM in the Italian Banking Industry

The study carried out by CeTIF[5] was undertaken in the banking industry, in banks of three different sizes: "major", "large", and "medium". Interviews with marketing and information systems managers were conducted with the aid of structured questionnaires. Twelve cases of interest were found, showing the approaches followed in creating CRM projects, the reference technologies employed, and the change management initiatives undertaken.

The following are the major results:

a) There is difficulty in identifying CRM unequivocally. In most cases, definitions were partial and referred only to certain aspects of CRM, technological aspects in particular.

b) Only in very few cases did the approach to CRM consider organizational problems, which on the contrary deeply affect bank processes and sales channels. Support for change processes in marketing and sales area was usually lacking.

c) It has to be noted, however, that the said perceptions, as well as following project approaches, are tightly connected to management specificity and available resources: only banks with commitment from high management view CRM as a factor in organizational innovation, and not simply as a sophisticated information tool.

d) CRM projects require a complete review of the attitude to customers and sales processes, and to the creation of new products and services.

e) None of the cases studied showed a completely concluded project. Most banks are presently busy creating some of the CRM components or integrating them with the *legacy systems*.

f) An evolution in competencies was found, which in some cases contributed to the birth of new roles and in others to adjustment of the existing ones (this particularly applied to marketing units). A birth of new roles was noticed in the information system area as well, roles deputed to promote actual integration and alignment among operational systems, which manage *tout court* relationships between customers and distribution channels.

g) In the banking industry there is still a huge lack in terms of customer relationship-related competencies.

---

[5] CeTIF is a leading research centre of the Management Faculty at the Catholic University of Milan focusing on organizational and IT issues in the banking industry instituted in 1990.

h) Definition of criteria for the evaluation of investment revenue of CRM projects was most uncommon.

i) Present project teams are mostly made up of persons with technological knowledge, which greatly limits CRM's strategic relevance.

2.10.1 The Most Interesting Cases

2.10.1.1 The Case of Comit Bank

Comit's[6] Financial Studies and Analyses Office (a branch of the Strategic Support Systems Development Section) has created a project (as a part of the bigger SPRINT project, which stands in Italian for Segment in Order to Achieve New Targets Together) aiming to show how an analytical CRM system can enhance and deepen familiarity with customers, increase target marketing efficiency, and put branch directors in charge of the customer portfolio.

During the said project, efforts have been made to point out how results can be attained without particular technological resources, thanks to interactivity with the domain expert and interactivity in the data mining approach. As a matter of fact, only the bank's usual analytical equipment was employed. The objective of the project was, in short, to demonstrate how the implementation of the system mentioned might represent an opportunity for increasing the number of tools available to knowledge creation and management, although on a small scale.

In fact, the first results emerging from Comit's project indicated that:

1. Activities that would lead to complete automation of knowledge extraction process are feasible only to a certain degree.

2. Massive organizational interventions, which are bound to upset many existing processes, are required.

3. There is a lot of space available for the creation of complete CRM systems aiming to automate activities that are closely related to the market. However, approaches are required to face the problem in an integrative way, in order to amplify the opportunities currently offered by technology.

4. Priority must be given to ensuring that the bank's information heritage undergoes deep restructuring that will allow making out customer reaction profiles for each product/service and distribution channel. One of Comit's major difficulties was that it had to operate through an informa-

---

[6] Comit has recently merged with Banca Intesa, the biggest Italian bank.

tion basis consisting exclusively of data on possession and consistency of products/services offered by the bank.

5. Use of statistical and data mining tools forced the bank to redefine internal competencies and to introduce new resources with sufficient skills so as to ensure project quality standards, with a view to aligning business and technology.

6. Comit's activities demonstrated how one of CRM's components is actually capable of enhancing knowledge of customers that has previously been ignored, through direct exploration of the bank's data heritage.

7. The management's commitment was important in this, as was the ability to combine business and technological competencies in a synergistic manner.

8. These applications lend support to management decision activities and enhance comprehension of dynamic phenomena through information that allows for proper exploitation and evaluation of domain competencies.

2.10.1.2 The case of Banca Monte Paschi di Siena (BMPS)

In the mid-1990s, BMPS decided to increase its market and customer orientation. It therefore started a revision of its internal organization; both central and peripheral, to make its products/services available through several different channels, with the purpose of achieving connected benefits, such as greater market coverage, cost reduction, and better knowledge of customers.

BMPS was conscious that it had to take steps to reinforce marketing and integrate channels, creating new structures, that would be able, unlike the traditional ones, to support the customer-centred strategic orientation, which was pointed out earlier and in which the client is the core.

As a consequence, BMPS's trend is a progressive conversion of its branches into "financial shops", where customers can find the answer to most of their needs. However, many of the activities performed appear to be more and more inconsistent with the final target (accounting, risk management, etc.) Technological investments were aimed at pulling the project together in such a way as to incorporate fewer value-added activities (especially back-office activities).

Subsequently, thanks to the new opportunities technology offers, BMPS decided to invest in virtual channels, so as to offer its customers services that do not imply a physical presence and are not restricted by time problems.

BMPS realized that, in order to achieve its goals, it had to concentrate on change management activities and that it would be faced with resistance and culture shock. Formerly, in 1992, it had already started restructuring of the distribution net, turning it from functional to divisional (i.e. per customer segment: private citizens and companies), and therefore retraining personnel: product experts became segment experts, and accountants/administrators became salesmen.

The next step was to design a marketing information system (which is part of an analytical CRM), its purpose being proper customer segmentation, so as to allow targeted marketing activities through enhanced customer intelligence and integration of systems and analysis tools. Owing to project realization difficulties, an internal organizational unit called "Channels and Customer Intelligence", able to marry up sales/marketing and technological competencies, had to be founded. The Systems function, shaped as an external consortium, only performed support services in alignment of legacy and marketing systems. Business intelligence systems (mainly data warehouse and data mining) and customer care centres sprang to life. At the end of the 1990s investments were also made in collaborative CRM, so as to make home banking and trading on-line services available and activate customer care initiatives, such as customer intelligence, call centres, and automatic branches.

Today BMPS has completed the installation of many of the CRM systems and is currently busy developing and integrating further services.

The problems encountered by BMPS while designing the mentioned projects were:

a) Internal:

   • Culture shock and speed of change (BMPS used to be focused on accounting/administrative problems and not on customer-oriented ones),

   • Alignment of business and technological competencies,

   • Realization of projects was hardly coherent with initial design (new problems were faced with old interpretation criteria).

b) External:

   • Providers merely offered innovative technological solutions, without taking care of internal problems triggered by change (which concerned both the bank and the market).

   • On the one hand the "actions" proposed by providers and consultants did not respect factors peculiar to the internal environment (owing to a poor internal analysis), and on the other hand, they were "aseptic" compared with the magnitude of the changes required (there was no agreement about what way to take to achieve targets).

2.11 Conclusions

With reference to what has been said above and to the initial results of our research, CRM can be considered as a number of activities aiming to overturn the temporal sequence in interaction between company and environment. It allows, in fact, mitigation of industry and market impacts (environmental repercussions in short) by creating a more stable and efficient technical core. A transfer of design/production activities takes place from the technical core to the boundary-spanning component. In other words, CRM causes a sharper definition of the boundary line between the two subsystems, moving activities from the "engine room" to the areas assigned to customer relationship organization and management (as shown in Fig. 2.4).

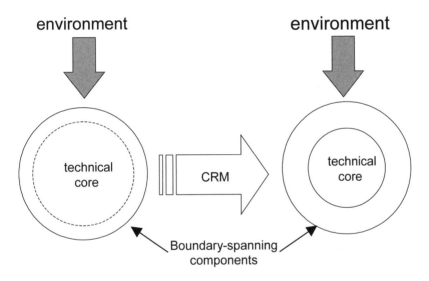

Figure 2.4   Technical core and CRM

As a consequence, there is a reduction of the boundary-spanning component and a trend towards increased activity standardization and thus increased efficiency, which will promote growth in the units that manage and organize customer interaction.

For the same reasons, such initiatives drive technological competencies from information systems units to sales/marketing units. That is how "marketing information systems" competency areas are born: they are dependent hierarchically on the marketing unit and embrace business and technological knowledge, clearly showing, perhaps for the first time, the alignment between business and technology.

3 The Organization of Data Warehouse Activities

3.1 Introduction

In the last decade, the configuration of the banking market has seen a steady increase in competition levels,[7] owing to the relaxation of restrictions on banks' operational independence, to the entry of nonbanking operators into the payments system, and to the banks' new role in the financial market (Banca d'Italia, 1996).

This market transformation has stimulated the whole banking brokerage industry and pushed it in the direction of supporting innovation in the services provided through the increasingly more systematic and coordinated use of information technology.

In this context, banks are affected by changes in environment, market, and regulations as well as by the opportunities offered by technology, and they have therefore reacted by increasing their own technical resources.

It might be added that the inherent nature of banking services, which is primarily informative, is conducive to recourse to information technologies[8] on a massive scale (Porter, Millar, 1985).

As a matter of fact, the use of IT is of fundamental importance to banks, not just for processing the huge amounts of data they hold or to carry out on-line transac-

---

[7] We refer to the innovations introduced by EU directives on banking coordination, and, in Italy's particular case, to the new overall regulation system for the banking industry.

[8] Porter and Millar (1985) in *How Information Gives You Competitive Advantages,* classify different industrial sectors through an information intensity matrix. The said matrix allows analysis of the needs in terms of information intensity of processes and contents for the products/services typical of each sector. They then give an evaluation of existing and potential information intensities of processes and products, stating that these can determine role and dimension of IT in every industrial sector. Porter and Millar demonstrate how IT is a fundamental variable in all activities carried out by the bank. They do this by focusing on the needs and information contents typical of the banking sector which, in order to fulfil its objectives, uses IT in a consistent and systematic way. They thus conclude by saying the high information contents in products/services and the high information intensity in processes make the banking sector one of the most enthusiastic in the use of IT. On the same issue see also Rossignoli (1997).

tions, or yet to execute processes: it is also vital to enhancement of the decision-making process.

Although technological innovation has long provided banks with tools that can facilitate production processes, there does not appear to have been a corresponding evolution in decision process support systems.

In other words, we have a massive use of IT in the automation of operational activities, contrasting with scant use of effective decision support systems.

Banks and financial institutions have been using information systems for decades in the automation of strictly operative or operational activities. System architecture and archive structure were usually designed to increase process efficiency. Therefore, memorizing modes and data access were meant to support the operational activity only, limiting the reuse of the same data for decisional purposes.

In recent years, there has been an attempt to use the available data to produce the information necessary to enhance stringency, consistency and reliability in decision process management. (CIPA/ABI, 1999).

Traditional systems have proved ineffective in responding to decisional needs. New approaches to coping with the inadequacy of traditional information technology have come up over time: among these, the business intelligence systems, particularly data warehousing and data mining, seem to be outstanding in the enhancement of decision processes.[9]

The aim of the present work is to give an overall conceptual view, from the perspective of an integration between the traditional, transaction-oriented information system and the new, decision-oriented one, while highlighting the potentials of data warehousing and data mining in the banking industry.

3.2   The Data Warehouse

The operational information system supports the company's mission critical activities. However, it does not allow data processing for objectives other than transactions. The reason is in most cases the lack of a platform integrated with the in-

---

[9] It is interesting to remark that artificial intelligence systems, which are now included in data mining systems, are a technology that was already available in the 1950s. However, they   partly owing to a natural reaction of resistance to change among management, partly because of the high implementation costs, and partly because of technical factors making it impossible to implement them, such as difficulties in accessing and reusing company data.

formation system that is able to direct elaboration processes in order to obtain the desired information to support decision-making.

Owing to an increasingly globalized and competitive market, new needs are coming up in the banking industry, such as the need to provide integrated information in an easy language (not system or technical language), the coordination of the company's activities in presenting data that cross technical and organizational boundaries, or again the availability of historical (and usable) data for analysis of the events (Rajola, 2000).

Owing to market drive, which promotes the development of new products and services, the diffusion of these through advanced marketing systems, and the evaluation of their profitability, there is a growing interest of banks toward the implementation of new technologies for strategic support (Banca d'Italia, 1996).[10]

It must be noted from the start that application areas for planning, control, and generally execution of information systems are still weak, owing to the rather traditional views of banks' boards.

However, for a few years now the objective of information technology wizards has been the integration of system legacy applications with decision support systems.

In view of this, and in spite of different approaches in the past,[11] it dawned on the study group that the experiments undertaken were failing to yield any satisfactory results, and above all, were unable to provide concrete advantages within the schedule (De Marco, 1997).

During the last few years a new approach has been taking over: the data warehouse. Such an approach is proving to be an excellent way to move the limit of operational elaboration into the decision area.

There are many motivations that lead companies, especially financial institutions, to create a data warehouse. By this means they certainly aim to:

---

[10] On this issue, CeTIF carried out a research study in . Forty banks of different sizes were involved (accounting at the time for 50% of the profits of the entire banking sector). Five different areas were explored: control over several sectors of the financing area, management control, management information system, strategic planning and ALM (Asset and Liability Management). It emerged from the results that while in the first two sectors information systems enjoyed a certain, if not sufficient, diffusion, the third and fourth areas had a limited use for such tools, since many activities were still performed by hand and in the fifth there was an extremely low spread of information systems, because there were few companies implementing innovations.

[11] Such as data modelling, information engineering, and other approaches.

- Research opportunities for growth,

- Create internal efficiency,

- Contain costs,

- Support strategic decisions.

The data warehouse is a tool that makes it possible to spot opportunities for growth and to exploit the current change processes as far as possible.

It guarantees data quality and reliability and thus creates a common certified information base to draw from. What is more, it permits highlighting of data inter-relations, favouring teamwork. In short, it promotes the coordination of activities and internal efficiency (Cash, McFarlan, McKenney, 1998; Ciborra, 2000; Dyché, 2000).

Cost containment is a medium-/long-term objective that cannot be achieved until the whole warehouse structure is complete. In particular, the main aspects leading to cost containment concern single customer profitability, product/service potentials in terms of profitability and generated cost structure, and the spotting of targeted, highly successful marketing campaigns (Brown, 2000).

The data warehouse allows powerful synthesis and the analysis function. The analysis function allows significant information to be spotted among the huge amount of information present in banking systems; it is a synthesis tool owing to its ability to highlight macro-information starting from synthesis data. Therefore, it can provide the management with aggregate data, while enabling it to navigate within the data themselves, in order to obtain analytical information (Kelly, 1997; Kimball, 1996).

The strategic and decisional use of the data warehouse (DWH) consequently range from the company's global positioning to the placement of reference products/services, and from customer profile analysis to the profitability analysis of the business in which the company operates.

3.3   A Definition of Data Warehouse

In spite of the popularity the acronym DWH has enjoyed in the last few years, bringing many companies to implement (or to plan the implementation of) DWH systems, there is still no unanimously accepted definition of 'data warehouse'.

For some authors, DWH is simply a synonym for a physical database (relational or multidimensional) containing data. According to other authors, it can be defined as an environment with data structures meant for decision support, which is physically separated from the operational systems. However, both definitions appear to be limited, and neither can explain the concept as a whole.

Inmon, the first author who referred explicitly to data warehouse, defines it instead as an **integrated** data collection, which is *subject oriented, time variant* and *nonvolatile* and which supports decision processes (Inmon, 1996). Therefore, data integration is a necessary requirement for an adequate design, and sets the DWH apart from any other decision support system.

According to Inmon, the data collection is:

- Integrated

  This is the fundamental requirement. Data from several operational systems and other external sources flow into the data warehouse. There are different ways to achieve such integration: using uniform coding methods, ensuring semantic homogeneity of all variables, or using the same measurement units (e.g. day-month-year).

- Subject oriented

  The DWH is oriented to specific company issues (e.g. customers, products, etc.) rather than to functions or applications (e.g. operational applications in the banking context). Data are stored to allow easy reading and elaboration by the users. Therefore, the objective is not to minimize redundancy through normalization, but to provide structured data that are able to foster information production.

  There is a transition from function-oriented design to data modelling, in order to create a multidimensional view of the data themselves (Inmon, 1996; Kimball, 1996).

- Time variant

  The data stored in the DWH have a much wider time horizon than those contained in an operational system. In the DWH there is an amount of information concerning areas of interest, which outline the situation of a given phenomenon along a given period, which is rather long. As a consequence, the data are updated to a certain date, which is generally prior to the interview with the user (Inmon, 1996).

- Nonvolatile

  The data contained in the DWH are nonmodifiable, access being permitted only for reading. This allows for a simpler design than needed for a relational database, supporting an operational application. In this context, possible malfunctions due to updating do not have to be faced, and much less is there a need for complex tools to manage the referential integrity or to block records being updated from user access.

In short, the DWH describes the acquisition, transformation, and distribution processes of the information present inside or outside[12] the company, as a support to decision makers.

Therefore, it stands apart from all other management systems which, in contrast, are simply aimed at automation of routine operations. Table 3.1 shows the main differences between an operational system and a DWH.

Table 3.1   Source: Kelly S., Data Warehousing in Action, 1997.

	DWH	TRADITIONAL SYSTEM
Use	*Query intensive*	*Transaction intensive*
Users	Fairly small number	Fairly large number
Data historicity	Historical and current data	Current data
Integration	Subject oriented	Limited activities or process
Data quality	In terms of data consistency	In terms of data integrity
Database	Updating at predefined intervals, therefore *nonvolatile*	Constant updating, therefore *volatile*
Data model	Generally denormalized data; the model conforming to the size of the subject	Normalized data; the model conforming to the needs originating from supported transactions
Application domain	DWH projects provide an infrastructure to decision support systems, featuring scalability, extensibility and flexibility	Defined for a limited application range, referring to a specific application

---

[12] In this case we refer to data contained in company archives and to data coming from information providers, or from the Internet, or from the banking system in general.

Development	Development criteria respond to evolutionary and repetitive principles	OLTP[13] systems developed according to users' requirements and waterfall develop method
Sponsorship	A DWH project requires a strong sponsorship due to the organizational width	Operational systems tend to be sponsored following a clear process that allows to spot the foreman, who in his turn defines the organizational hierarchy

It must also be remarked that Inmon's definition introduces a concept of absolute indifference toward the architectural characteristics of operational systems and the physical location of the data in the different databases.

If the focus is set on the ability to support decisions, the DWH can be created in several different ways, ranging from a completely centralized logic (a single database accessed by all users) to a completely distributed logic (e.g. producing data copies in heterogeneous technical and functional environments).

3.3.1   Components and Architecture of a DWH

Figure 3.1 shows an example of a general DWH architecture. The main components of this are:

1. Data coming from the operational systems,

2. Data movements,

3. Data warehouse,

4. Metadata,

5. End-user.

Data coming from operational systems

These are the data processed by the bank's operational systems. They can be contained in the same database or originate from other databases, even external ones. The architecture often sees to the integration of internal and external data. The use of the latter allows enriching the information bulk.[14]

---

[13] *On Line Transaction Processing.* It refers to on-line-updated operational systems.

[14] An example is supplied by the data on a certain geographical area, or data from the Risk Centre, or those originating from information providers such as Reuters or Bloomberg.

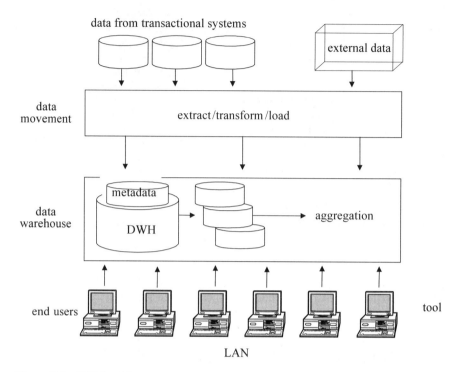

Figure 3.1 DWH architecture

Data movement

This component is responsible for data extraction from the operational systems, integration of internal and external data, preprocessing, consistency control, structure conversion, and updating of data dictionaries.

The data warehouse

After extraction from the operational systems, data are stored in the data warehouse. Here access is allowed only for reading purposes. DWH data have a historical dimension and refer to business subjects.

They can be stored in a central repository or in a datamart.

The term "datamart" is used to identify a "smaller" DWH designed to support a particular area of activities.[15] Think about the marketing datamart, where data

---

[15] Sometimes „datamart" is used to mean a number of decision support systems, isolated from one another and oriented to specific business problems. On other occasions the term is used to refer to server-based, local applications, which are fed by a central DWH. They are also called subsidiary datamarts.

filtered from the operational systems are stored to support customer analysis and other marketing activities. Therefore, it is possible to have several datamarts in the same bank, with different objectives and oriented to different business areas (Rajola, 2000).[16] The data contained in the DWH can be aggregated and summarized to respond to specific information needs.

The metadata

The metadata are the additional information bases that enrich the data contained in the DWH. They are often called, in jargon, "data about data", with the origin, use, value, or function indicated (Kimball, 1996).

For this purpose, actual information catalogues are created. These are the files containing metadata. The catalogue gives the user indications about the nature of the data contained in the DWH, their semantic meaning, which archive they come from, and their historicity.

The end user

The data contained in the DWH are then presented to the end user, who thus has a number of tools available for processing, in order to produce the appropriate information. The tools may be simple report and query generators, graphic interfaces for data representation, or more complex data analysis systems.

3.4   Main Issues of the Implementation Process of a Data Warehouse

The implementation process is conditioned by a number of basic requirements.

The main critical success factors have proved to be the organizational and technological components. The technological component concerns the study of:

1. Processing platforms,
2. Workstation configuration,
3. Local network,
4. Choice of DBMS,
5. Client/server environment,
6. Application and software.

---

[16] It is possible to have a data mart for the loans area, one for the financial area, and so on.

The organizational component includes training of personnel, acquisition of personnel with adequate skills to manage and maintain the data warehouse, and planning of actions to be undertaken.

The training of the users is an especially important factor. As a matter of fact, it has to be borne in mind that end users are used to an operational system and lack the knowledge necessary to perform data analyses (McKeen, Smith, 1996).

While, on the one hand, the diffusion of graphic interfaces and user-friendly systems has encouraged the spread of analysis tools, thus rendering user training simpler, on the other hand there is often a lack of the knowledge necessary to undertake analysis of activities in such a way as to yield satisfactory results (Rossignoli, 1997).

It is also necessary to combine introduction of the DWH with the creation of new professional figures who are able to manage and maintain the system. (De Marco, 1992)

It often happens that management and maintenance of the system are outsourced to external companies. This, however, cannot free the company from having at least one professional figure able to manage the relationship with providers from inside and future developments of the system. (Earl, 1996; Mayes, 2001; McFarlan, Nolan, 1995; Virtuani, 1997)

Another organizational component concerns the proper planning and management of the actions to be undertaken. For this purpose, it is necessary to define:

1. Modes of extraction and updating of DWH data,

2. Access modes and corresponding security levels (access through stratified passwords, one for each user, so as to guarantee proper privacy),

3. Management of metadata.

3.5   Organization of Warehousing Initiatives for Marketing Activities in the Banking Industry

Since the introduction of DWH and unstructured data analysis systems, with accumulating experience and data availability it has now become possible to forecast customers' needs. For this purpose it is necessary for the companies to focus their attention less on the increasing market share and more on each customer's share (Brown, 2000; Berson, Smith, Thearling, 2000).

The marketing database consists in using the information about customers to develop and keep up relations with them. When directed by events, marketing adds the crucial element of time. From the approach, "Here is the product; do you want to buy it?" the bank passes on to, "Here is a customer: what should I sell him? When should I sell it to him? and Which channel should I use to communicate with him?" Thus, the bank needs to be able to offer its customers a product/service that is suitable to fulfill his potential needs by even identifying the best distributive channel at the same time (Imhoff, Loftis, Geiger, 2001).

The success of a marketing campaign depends heavily on the degree of personalization which the operation is carried out with. However, except for a limited number of important customers, this activity is not commercially practicable. Somehow, business rules must be defined that might apply to several customers but at the same time give them the impression of satisfying their specific needs. In other words, it is necessary to define a segmentation of customers, which might make it easier to understand each customer's developing dynamics and attitudes (Morris, 2002; Bielski, 2001).

A real tendency towards the market means the definition of an offer focused on the needs of various customer segments, strategic and personalized communication, diversified structure of channels and so on (Scott, 1997). A tendency towards a customer is primarily based on advanced systems of organization, analysis and use of the information about customers and market in general. In this order, advanced competences and tools are necessary with regard to acquisition, analysis and use of the market information. It is also necessary to have a marketing intelligence, i.e. a constant market monitoring system, both strategic and executive. Such a system must be able to support the following main functions, to be evenly developed in strict correlation and coherence among themselves:

1. Acquisition of internal and external data,

2. Analysis and interpretation of data and of the phenomena they refer to,

3. Use of data and relevant information in the decisional process.

Through familiarity with the customers it is not only possible to identify the most interesting targets but also to understand how the working scenario develops, making it easier to direct the commercial action towards specific segments in a dominant way (Camuffo, Costa, 1995).

To cope with such needs it is useful to have and use a group of tools such as scoring cards, profiles and events. Scoring card models can include:

1. Models of relation's economic value (i.e. high value, low value),

2. Models of preferences for products' purchased, with lists of related events,

3. Preference models of sales channel.

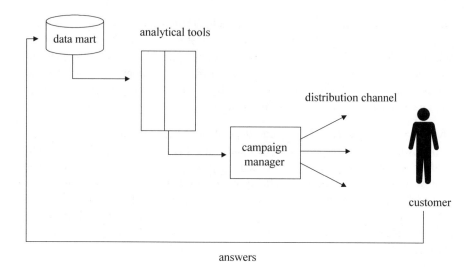

Figure 3.2. Main components of an integrated database marketing solution

Profiles and segments represent customers' groups usually characterized by similar behaviours and sufficient differences from customers belonging to other groups. They can be based either on the *status* (i.e. pensioners, married, with children, etc.) or on product use, or on a combination of both.

The main components of an integrated database marketing solution are:

1. A customer-oriented database (datamart for marketing),

2. Analytical tools (traditional systems, query and reporting, OLAP and data mining systems),

3. Campaign manager,

4. Distribution channels,

5. Tools to store events (answering memorization tools).

The customer data mart or database must contain all available data, which are organized around the customer himself, usually in a data mart if marketing is concerned. Though marketing campaigns may have the family or the product as a target, most communications are directed at individual customers, which is why the database has to be customer centred.

There are a number of analysis systems available for pattern recognition, linear regression, decision trees, neural nets, rule induction, genetic algorithms, and generally speaking, for all other data mining systems. The use of such analysis systems makes it possible to obtain several sets of rules that are suitable for picking out customer groups or group behaviours (Groth, 1998; Cranford, 1998; De Marco, 1997).

The campaign manager will then integrate the information (e.g. with the scoring paper concerning buying inclination) and create various campaigns using different combinations of his customer data (De Marco, 2002).

Distribution channels (such as call centres, branches, financial promoters, mail, Internet, ATMs) can be identified by the campaign manager and also represent the different ways through which products and services are offered to the customer.

In order to personalize future communications, it is important to keep a record of the customer's response to an offer. Though it is easy to ascertain whether the customer has bought a product shortly after the communication, it will be more difficult to evaluate his behaviour a long time after the offer.

As already said, one of the crucial points in a successful marketing operation is the consistency of the customer data. It has to be stressed that the customers' registrations are often taken from operational systems that are not up to date. In addition, owing to the great number of merger or acquisition (M&A) operations, the management of registration archives is apt to grow more and more difficult. M&A operations can nevertheless provide occasion for a thorough data review. In fact, it is possible to make provision for complete data "cleansing" and restructuring during the conversion and alignment of the information systems involved in a merger. In other words, in order to withstand competition, the systems and structures currently available to Italian banks urgently need to be reorganized, from the aspects of both structure and internal competence, to allow the most efficient use possible of them (Scott, 1997).

For instance, if the organization is aware of a customer's life cycle, or at least data such as the customer's profession, his income, or the ages of his children, it has an real advantage in customizing its services. These data can be obtained through questionnaires or product request forms. Customers are used to answering such questions for any kind of nonbanking product. It is thus important to recognize the value of this kind of information and to modify organizational procedures in order to acquire data and keep them up to date.

Another difficulty concerns access of marketing users to data contained in operational systems. Once such difficulty was acknowledged, some banks created a firm warehouse and used it as a platform for database marketing. Other enterprises have created a separate marketing database (some times a datamart), its data coming from the firm data warehouse or directly from the operational systems. We have here a marketing information system, run almost entirely by the marketing section, which has provided for integration of operational data with external sources and campaign results for each individual customer.

The marketing section can also add an organizing team including informatics experts to its staff and put it in charge management and development of its own departmental information system. It must be considered, though, that in many cases, data warehouse projects have failed to meet customers' expectations. The following chapters analyse the main conditions necessary to ensure the success of a warehouse project.

A brief example of customer analysis is now appropriate, to make this point clearer.

An analysis can show that a certain cluster of customers is interested in a given product. Conversely, if any customer has already stated that he is not interested in that specific product or that he owns it already, this information becomes more important than the results of the data analysis. A system capable of delivering such information must thus integrate both the analysis results and the answers formerly given by the customer.

This is just to show that customer-focused marketing not only requires knowledge of the products the customer already owns, but also calls for a *milieu,* equipped with memory for distribution channels as well, in order to create a dialogue with the customer over time.

It is hence useful to integrate marketing communications and all distribution channels.

Branch systems in particular should allow the operator to adjust information activities to the different kinds of event. This means that the operator will need multifunctional information support to allow him diversified and integrated management of his activities (bank teller activities, consulting, marketing, etc.) (Camuffo, Costa, 1995). For instance, in order to carry out branch marketing activities it is necessary that the system is able to manage both the sales message and the customer's response. One of this channel's advantages is immediate interaction: the customer visits the branch to carry out an operation, and the marketing message is handed to him as part of the process. In home banking too, the message can be part of the process when the customer enters his request. ATMs can also be a distribution channel, through presentation of communications thought to be of interest for the individual customer during waiting times.

We must consider the spread of alternative distribution channels and operativeness analysis of each single customer. Business intelligence systems now make it possible to spot purchase inclination in real time from behaviour characteristics and product/service, thus dynamically defining an information push directed at the individual customer (Carignani, 2001).

3.5.1 Case Studies

The following case studies reflect experience of the application of business intelli-gence systems in some of the major international institutions in the finance industry.

Midland Bank

Midland Bank, now acquired by HSBC, used scoring techniques, campaign test design, and test-and-campaign evaluation to carry out customer segmentation and targeting.

The targeting techniques used customer and external data together with a promo-tion campaign and came up with a method that singles out the importance of indi-vidual data; they combined these to produce a scoring formula, linked scoring val-ues with purchase inclination, tested the formula on new data, and finally used the formula on a large scale.

The campaign test evaluated and optimized the use of alternative offering strate-gies and identified the customer group for which each particular strategy was the optimum. In this way, in this campaign the best strategy could be used for each customer, instead of the one that brings the best results overall.

First Direct

First Direct used its marketing database to offer its customers personal loans, credit cards, high-interest deposits, and stock exchange products.

By means of scoring cards and an accurate campaign test strategy, First Direct has doubled its response rates and sales volume; it has also increased customer knowl-edge, identifying the most profitable customers, and has enhanced its relational marketing culture.

Bank of Scotland

Although customers were generally satisfied with the service provided, Bank of Scotland recognized that there was a risk of the most sophisticated, who are usu-ally also the most profitable, switching to rival banks. Therefore, it tried to prove its ability to provide better services than its competitors. To this end, it created a strategic analysis unit, originally composed of 28 members. The members are market analysts, planners, researchers, statistic experts and data modellers. The unit is active in four different areas: data quality, database marketing, relational marketing and market research.

The marketing database is based on a company warehouse. The relational market-ing group, which produces profiles, samples, and targets, uses it and analyses campaign effectiveness. The data quality group makes sure that the data are correct and are kept up to date.

In 1992 the pilot project started, with six branches involved and using a commercially available package. In 1994, a complete marketing database was created by copying the customer database and adding several data; the package was later extended to the whole bank.

The branches spot the customers involved in a campaign and can thus offer products and file customer answers. The statistical analysis is performed on the marketing database. A marketing datamart that is to contain all data necessary for statistical analyses is currently under construction. A geographic information system is also used, so that campaign results can be presented for each branch.

The bank is soon to start event-driven campaigns. It is also developing models designed to make it possible to forecast what products will be purchased first by customers.

Key benefits of the package are campaign control and coordination, the ability to manage very large amounts of data, event management, definition of complex market clusters, the analysis capability, and the history of all campaigns implemented on each customer.

Canadian Imperial Bank of Commerce

The Canadian Imperial Bank of Commerce (CIBS) converted its entire operational database into a data warehouse, creating an information base to be used for effective management of both credit risk and market risk.

The system aims both to integrate the data at a global level and to standardize activities in the different markets.

The main business objective achieved was the enhancement of risk management, because the bank achieved a better rank position on the financial markets.

Wells Fargo Bank

Wells Fargo Bank (WFB) created a centralized data warehouse consisting of several datamarts. The system is automatically fed by the operational system. The application areas covered by the data warehouse include marketing, customer management, and operational reporting. The data warehouse was enriched and completed in time through integration of the data contained in the operational systems of the banks acquired by WFB. For instance, the acquisition of *First Interstate* triggered a project aiming to rationalize the sales network. The first step, besides the integration of the entire information system, was the appropriation of *First Interstate*'s data to feed the centralized data warehouse. The creation of a single data warehouse allowed performance of an analysis aimed at spotting the characteristics of each branch. This analysis, in turn, made it possible to obtain profitability rate, number of nonloyal customers, and profitability of individual customers for each branch. In this way the bank was able to evaluate the costs and benefits that would accrue from the closure of each branch, thus enhancing the rationalization process of the whole sales network.

Such a system was later used to evaluate the profitability of all the bank's customers and spot the potentially better ones.

Capital One

Within Capital One, more than 50 persons were appointed to posts dedicated to the creation of the data warehouse. In this warehouse more than 3 TB of data are held, including data on about 7 million accounts. The system is aimed at identifying new customers and creating new products that will be offered to the most profitable customer clusters. Through the analysis of the data contained in the data warehouse, Capital One is able to launch promotional campaigns and to verify the redemption of these per market, geographic area and customer cluster to which the campaign itself was addressed, all within a few weeks.

Capital One is also in a position to perform mass customization policies in the offer of retail and wholesale products.

Thanks to this initiative, Capital One is considered one of North America's most flexible and innovative banks.

First National Bank of Chicago

Because of the interest shown by its financial area, the First National Bank of Chicago, one of the major banks of America, started a data warehouse project.

The objective was to create a system that would be able to rationalize management costs through more accurate planning of future actions and report activities. The system, which amounts to nearly 2 TB, can offer its features to 400 users.

It fulfils four distinct requirements defined by the users:

1. Enrichment of archives with metadata able to explain data and table contents,

2. Availability of data on demand,

3. Electronic delivery and accessibility,

4. Report standardization.

The data that flowed into the warehouse and were necessary to respond to user requirements originated from eight distinct legacy systems. Data integration was carried out through definition of ten characteristics the system had to respond to:

1. Common key elements,

2. Coherent data definition,

3. Rational data transformation,

4. Synchronization of acquisition terms,

5. Ability to navigate among the data through the use of metadata,

6. Electronic information delivery,

7. Automatic data aggregation,

8. System based on a client/server mainframe architecture,

9. Flexible architecture,

10. Centralized data source of financial movements.

While implementing the project, First Chicago paid particular attention to new organizational settings, training for the personnel involved, and change management problems.

First USA

First USA is the third VISA and MasterCard credit cards issuer in the United States. It implemented a data warehouse holding over 2 TB of data. The greatest business driver for First USA was the increase of its market share. Therefore, it chose to identify the potentially most profitable customers and to offer new products and services to the high-value clusters.

4 Organization of Knowledge Discovery and Customer Insight Activities

Banking transactions require storage and processing of large amounts of data. Knowledge discovery processes allow analysis of such data with the aim of spotting complex behaviour patterns and characteristics of the variables contained in the archives. Knowledge discovery processes and data mining systems can be used in a wide range of financial applications.

The most popular applications that use systems based on knowledge discovery processes are the market-oriented ones. However, these systems are also successfully employed in other application domains. They are in fact used for fraud detection, in the identification of wrongful behaviour concerning credit cards in the case of theft or forgery; in addition they are also used to minimize loan risks and again to evaluate customer value.

The fundamental steps in knowledge discovery process and data mining systems are summarized below.

4.1 Knowledge Discovery Process

The terms "KDD" (knowledge discovery in database) and "data mining" are often used as synonyms.

KDD means the entire process of identification and extraction of significant and potentially useful reality interpretative models that are necessary to generate knowledge.

Data mining, on the other hand, refers to the application of algorithms in order to extract models or behaviour rules from the data, and to correct interpretation of the results. Therefore, it represents one phase of the knowledge discovery process (figure 4.1).

KDD is the next analysis level after statistical computations (Fayyad, Shapiro, 1996). KDD is represented by a large number of algorithms searching for particular relationships between data in the absence of any a priori hypotheses. The analysis approach is therefore totally data driven. Analysis complexity is at its greatest, and processing time is consistently very long.

The knowledge discovery process is a repetitive and interactive process (Fayyad, Shapiro, 1996; Rajola, 2000), which requires the user to go through numerous stages before managing to "discover knowledge". Such a process can be summarized as follows:

1. Definition and understanding of the application domain and definition of the business objectives to be achieved.

2. Creation of a *target data set*: selection of a *subset* of variables and data or sampling of data to be used in the knowledge discovery process.

3. *Data cleansing* and *preprocessing:* fundamental operations to reduce the presence of noise in the data, or of the *outliers* if necessary, selection of the information needed to create the model, decision on attitude to missing or incomplete fields and on the data's historical dimension, and definition of updating modes.

4. *Data reduction* and *projection:* definition of data representation modes with reference to the targets to be achieved. Use of transformation methods to reduce variables.

5. Choice of the role of data mining in the analysis: use of data mining systems for classification, regression, clustering, etc.

6. Choice of data mining tools: selection of methods to be used for pattern research. Such a choice also requires a decision on which models or parameters might be more appropriate. Integration of the data mining methods selected in the entire knowledge discovery process (Berson, Smith, Thearling, 2000; Delmater, Hancok, 2001).

7. Data mining: research of models of interest to the user and their presentation according to predefined modes: classification, rule induction, decision tree, regression, cluster definition, etc. The user can interact with the system in order to refine each outcome (Lee, 2000; Poe, 1996; Rossignoli, 1993).

8. Interpretation of identified models, possible retroaction at previous points for further iterations.

9. Consolidation of knowledge discovered: integration of this and evaluation of system performance. Supply of the documentation to end users and interested third parties.

It is important to point out that the process does not end with a single iteration. On the contrary, it calls for continuous refinement of the results obtained, in order to progress to the creation of a pattern that allows the interpretation of the phenomena that are the object of the analysis.

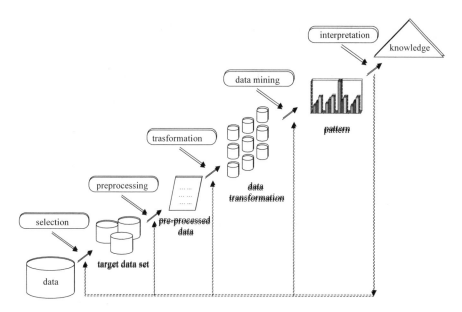

Figure 4.1   Knowledge discovery in database (KDD) process. Source: Fayyad–Shapiro, 1996

The knowledge discovery process might require a significant number of iterations, as shown by the dotted lines in Figure 4.1. It might even create loops between two or more phases. Figure 4.1 shows the fundamental steps in reaching the stage of discovering knowledge. It also gives an impression of the possible loops between the different stages.

After this brief summary of the fundamental points of the knowledge discovery process, we will now focus our attention on data mining systems.

4.2   Data Mining

Definition and understanding of the business objectives and the application domain are the first stage in the knowledge discovery process. It requires spotting the business objectives to which the system is to be applied, as in the analysis stage of a traditional system. The objective is to make the users' requirements and the system's specifications explicit. However, it has to be remarked that, while in the life cycle analysis of an information system it is possible to define the underlying algorithms specifically, this is not the case in the knowledge discovery process. For instance, in the creation of a warehouse management procedure, the flows, processes and automation rules are known or easy to find out. In contrast, in the creation of a knowledge discovery process it is possible to define the general objective, e.g. customer segmentation with a view to offering new products, clearly, whilst the appropriate algorithms that allow customer segmentation are not known and thus not cannot be explained. However, it is possible to single out the necessary data, their formatting modes, and a number of other characteristics needed for application of the techniques that allow clustering algorithms to be elaborated.

The next step is the creation of a target data set.

This stage includes exact identification of the amount of data to be used, the definition of the sampling methods when needed, and outlining of the data model to which the data mining techniques are to be applied (Berson, Smith, Thearling, 2000).

The amount of data necessary depends on the business objectives already defined. Internal and external data may be used.

The internal data are those already available to the company, either contained in archives specially set up to support the knowledge discovery process[17] or originating from other operational applications. In principle, in order to feed the decision support archives, criteria both for the extraction of data from the operational systems and for feeding modes for the databases used in the knowledge discovery process must be defined (Fig. 4.2).

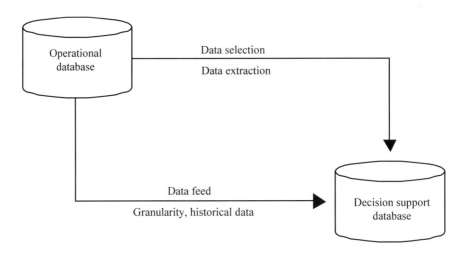

Figure 4.2   Decision support database

---

[17] We refer to a data warehouses, datamarts, or other, simpler, archives especially created to support the knowledge discovery process.

It is also necessary to define the historical dimension of the data (the time-lag necessary before the process can be carried out: for example at least 2 years of historical data would be needed to analyse a customer's behaviour and find out which set of products/services he might be interested in), the granularity and the insertion of elementary or aggregated data ahead of time.

Archives created for decision support can be integrated with data coming from external sources, such as information providers, the Internet, or market research companies. The reason for this choice is the enrichment and sometimes also the completion of the information bases to which the data mining systems will eventually be applied (Fig. 4.3). It is, however, necessary to ensure that the external data and the data contained in the decisional archives have the same structures.

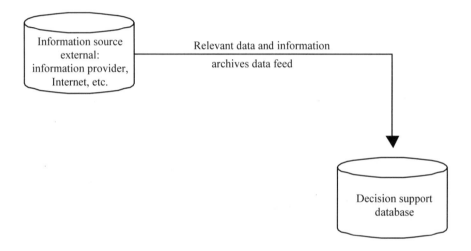

Figure 4.3   Relevant information and decision support database

Finally, the creation of a decision support database requires regular scheduling for updating times of the decisions (Berry, Linoff, 1999). Frequency and modes vary according to the application domain and to the dynamism of the environment within which the action takes place. For instance, the updating speed of a stock exchange index preview system has to be greater than one for a customer segmentation system. The variables of the former are sure to be more subject to changes than those of the latter.

It has to be noted, however, that traditional systems especially created for operational purposes or nonintegrated data sets are proving unable to support the decision process. New approaches have come out in order to face the limitations of traditional information technology in this field and nonintegrated data supports in general. A consolidated tendency, as already mentioned, is that of associating data mining systems with data warehouses. The latter can be defined as a source that is able to contribute to the enhancement of decision processes.[18] A general architecture of this is displayed here (Fig. 4.4). It shows briefly how data coming from the warehouse can be used to create data sets that can be used by data mining systems.

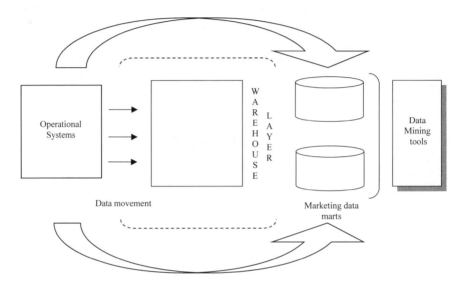

Figure 4.4 Data feed for data mining tools

The next phase is data cleaning and preprocessing.

This activity is tightly linked to the previous one. As previously noted, data can originate from operational systems, data warehouse or data mart. The intensity of the data cleansing and processing operations is higher if the reference data are directly extracted from the operational systems (Berson, Smith, Thearling, 2000). Otherwise, the intervention is certainly a limited one. Nevertheless, it has to be pointed out that if the "business subjects" (Inmon, 1996), i.e. those areas and activities specifically dedicated to the use of data analysis systems, have not been clearly defined in the realization phase, a data cleaning and preprocessing opera-

---

[18] As already mentioned, it must be noted that artificial intelligence systems, which are now incorporated in data mining systems, were already available technology back in the 1950s. However, they failed to catch on, owing partly to a natural resistance of company managements to change, partly to the high implementation costs, and partly also to technical impossibilities, such as difficulty in accessing and reusing company data.

tion will be required anyway. We need only think of the use of data mining systems for cross-selling activities. These require "certified" data, which can already be used by the systems described and with an aggregation level oriented to the objectives to be achieved (Groth, 1998).

Data cleansing and preprocessing are fundamental operations in order to:

1. Reduce the presence of data noise or, when necessary, of outliers,
2. Guarantee that the data are certified, i.e. updated and consistent,
3. Select the information necessary to create the model,
4. Decide how to treat empty or incomplete fields,
5. Define the historical dimension of the data to be treated; it is necessary to set a temporal interval common to all variables.

The subsequent data reduction and projection phase concerns the definition, linked to the objectives to be achieved, of data representation modes and, possibly, of transformation methods, in order to reduce the number of variables.

This is the moment to choose the role of the data mining systems in the analysis.

Data mining systems can be used to attain a number of different goals and should be related to the problems that are the object of the analysis, which can concern classification, clustering, sequencing, association and prediction (see Table 4.1).

Table 4.1   Problems that can be approached through data mining. Source: adapted by META Group, 1999

PROBLEMS	DEFINITION
Classification	Definition of data set characteristics
Clustering	Identification of the affinities defining groups in a data set that show similar behaviour and definition of common variables
Sequencing	Identification of correlation between behaviours within a pre-defined period
Association	Identification of correlation between behaviours that recur in the same period
Prediction	Identification of nonlinear trends based on historical data

The next step is to choose the data mining algorithm to be used in the process.

Once the role of the data mining systems in the analysis has been identified according to each application domain, it is possible to single out the data mining techniques to be used in the knowledge discovery process as a preliminary stage. Table 4.2 shows an example of the most popular techniques related to each kind of problem. However, it must be noted that the choice is not always the product of a direct relationship between the technique and the problem. The choice of data mining algorithms concerns the selection of the methods to use in pattern research in particular. Such a choice requires a decision on the more appropriate models or parameters.

In order to carry out the knowledge discovery process, it is sometimes necessary to combine several data mining techniques, while at other times it is best to switch the chosen techniques with others able to guarantee a better final result[19] (Berry, Linoff, 1999; Berry, Linoff, 1997).

Table 4.2   Most popular techniques for particular problems. Source: adapted by META Group, 1999

EXAMPLE	PROBLEM TYPE	RECOMMENDED TECHNIQUE
What are the three main reasons why my customer to switched to the competition?	Classification	Neural networks Decision tree
Which customer segments can I offer new products/ services to?	Clustering	Neural networks Decision tree
What are the odds that a customer who has opened an account will purchase product x in a short time?	Sequencing	Statistical techniques Rule induction
What are the odds that a customer might buy two entirely different products?	Association	Statistical techniques Rule induction
How much will the stock be worth in a day/year/etc.?	Prediction	Neural networks Statistical techniques

---

[19] For example, the user may be more interested in understanding the model than in originating a prediction.

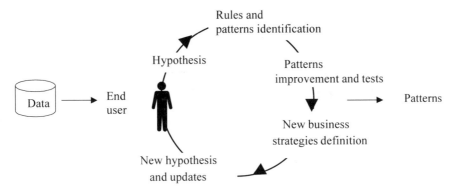

Figure 4.5   Interactions between end users and data mining tools. Source: Rajola, 2000

The main purpose is to look for models of interest to the user, presented according to predefined representation modes: rule induction (decision tree), regression, clustering, etc. The user can interact with the system to refine each outcome, and use several techniques to reach his objectives (Berry, Linoff, 1997). The use of the latter often requires extensive interaction to refine the obtained models. For instance, in the case of neural nets, the user defines a set of variables and the values of all the parameters. He is then forced to intervene in the parameters and variables to refine the analysis. This phase is characterized by a high degree of interactivity and interactivity between system and user. Figure 4.5 shows the process that leads to the creation of the model. It points out how, in subsequent steps, the user refines the rules that were spotted to create a model able to explain certain trends or phenomena.

Data mining is defined as the set of techniques that allows the exploration and analysis of data so that models, and logical schemes that are not explicit a priori, can be spotted within very large databases (Berry, Linoff, 1997; Rajola, 2000).

The data mining systems for model definition are used in two main ways: mixed initiative (both the system and the user) or fully automatic.

In the first case an intelligent process which automatically carries out the analysis, assists the user in presetting the following criteria and identifying significant patterns (see Figure 4.5). In the second case, the system discovers patterns through an automated model search with no need for user queries. In this case, the system allows for full automation of the data analysis process. It is able to carry out queries on its own. In order to discover information, it formulates a hypothesis, proposes a query and searches for its results, performs a statistical analysis on the obtained results, visualizes the results and finally modifies the hypotheses. The cycle goes on until an interpretation model is created. In the process, the system continually runs queries to the database, validating or rejecting partial results, until it finds a way of creating a pattern for a given behaviour (Rajola, 2000) (Figure 4.6).

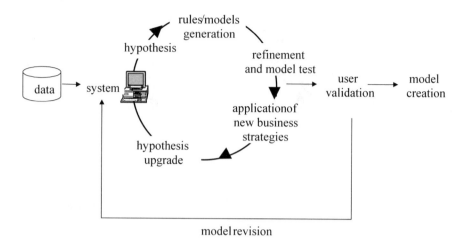

Figure 4.6   Generation of the model by the system itself. Source: Rajola, 2000

The following phase is an interpretation of results obtained, allowing appreciation of the quality of the model generated in general and of its underlying logic in particular. For instance, the use of Kohonen nets in marketing activities allows for segmentation of customers into homogeneous classes (Kohonen, 1990). However, it is not able to explain, or to point out clearly, which elements and/or rules attribute any particular customer to a particular class. The use of a rule induction system, applied to the results produced by the Kohonen net, generates a set of explicit rules showing the attribution criteria of customers to each class. In this way, the user is able to verify both the segmentation rules and the system's rate of reliability. What is more, he can, for instance, associate to each class the products he feels to be suitable for its needs (Berry, Linoff, 1997).

The final phase is knowledge production and consolidation. This is the last step in the knowledge discovery process. At this stage, the system is available to the users for achievement of their objectives. In the specific case, it acquires an operational value, for it allows application of the model to the reality of interest, in order to detect the actions to be carried out. To go back to the previous example, a marketing analyst uses the system both to associate each class with a range of products deemed suitable for the customers' needs and to estimate the marketing campaign's odds of success for each cluster (Stone, Woodcock, Machtynger, 2000). It might be added, for instance, that when a campaign manager is used it is possible to feed the databases or datamarts.

5 Data Mining Techniques

5.1 Introduction

Data mining, as already noted, is a component of the knowledge discovery process. It can be defined as a set of techniques that allows data analysis and exploration in order to discover significant rules or hidden models within large archives by means of an entirely or partially automated procedure (Berry, Linoff, 1997).

Therefore, this is a multidisciplinary approach unifying several techniques, such as statistics, visualization, knowledge-based systems and self-learning systems, that allow knowledge to be discovered and translated into rules and models that will be useful for business problem solving (Figure 5.1).

The objective of data mining systems is to enhance the knowledge process in all company areas and to reduce uncertainties in decision-making (Berry, Linoff, 1997; Kimball, 1996; Berson, Smith, Thearling, 2000).

As for every other information system, it is necessary to start from an accurate analysis of business needs. The user must be involved in all stages of the system's creation, for, besides verifying user requirements it is necessary to validate the results obtained and determine their quality (Adriaans, Zantinge, 1996). This aspect must not be neglected. In the creation of operational systems, it is usually possible to detect a process or algorithms and thus proceed with the subsequent

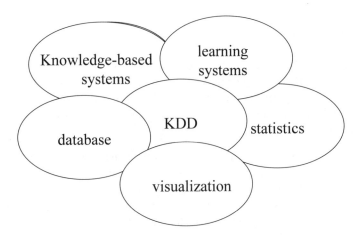

Figure 5.1   Data mining's multidisciplinary approach. Source: Adrianns–Zantige, 1996

phases of the automation, whereas in the creation of business intelligence, particularly data mining systems, the point is precisely to determine those underlying algorithms. Once the behaviour patterns are defined, it is necessary to undertake a multistep verification of them, so that they can be progressively refined and an effective system can be implemented (Adriaans, Zantinge, 1996).

Data mining systems can be used for model definition in two different ways: mixed initiative (the user's or the system's) or automatic.

5.2   The Most Prominent Data Mining Systems

As previously noted, there are several data mining techniques. Which one is used to solve business problems varies according to the application domain within which the analysis is to take place. The reader is referred to the tables in the previous chapter for more information on this matter. Though the market offers a large range of algorithms, these are the principal and most innovative data mining techniques (Adriaans, Zantinge, 1996):

1. Visualization,
2. Neural networks,
3. Genetic algorithms,
4. Fuzzy logic,
5. Rule induction and decision trees,
6. Cluster analysis.

5.3   Visualization

Several authors, when discussing visualization, allude to *Gestalt* theory. According to this, a *gestalt* is an organized entity or a whole, whose parts, though distinguishable, are interdependent. Some of their characteristics come from their inclusion in the whole, and the whole bears characteristics that are not to be found in any of the parts.

Data visualization techniques are methods used for pattern discovery within a given data set. The user interrogating a datamart or a data warehouse creates the data set. Such techniques may be used at the beginning of a data mining process for gross verification of the consistency and quality of the data, or for interpretation of the outcome of an analysis performed through other data mining techniques.

Visualization is a "transversal" system suitable for phenomena comprehension objectives (even dynamic ones), data analysis support, association to Q&R (query and reporting) systems, EIS (executive information system), statistical analyses, and neural nets.

Visualization allows analyses to be carried out on the correlation between variables, analyses on time series, and identification of patterns, spotting of anomalies, segment and cluster analysis, and territorial analysis.

Some visualization systems available on the market allow representation of up to twelve dimensions in a simple graph[20] (see Figs. 5.2, 5.3, 5.4). Figure 5.2 shows correlations found between different variables (financial, commercial, organizational, etc.) of hundreds of bank branches by using interpolations and different layers. Figure 5.3 represents an analysis concerning the spotting of operational anomalies throughout the branches of an important Italian banking group. Figure 5.4 displays an analysis of the distribution among clusters of a bank's customers. Such an analysis allows identification of the reaction of the customer classes to certain offered services.

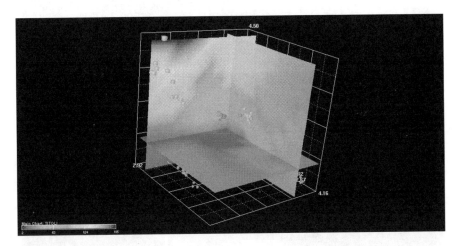

Figure 5.2   Visual analysis: correlation

---

[20] The graphic representations were developed for the DBInspector project, which was financed by the EC under the Esprit programme. Partners in the project were: the Bank of Italy, Southampton University's Parallel Applications Centre, the Centre for Information and Financing Technologies of the Università Cattolica del Sacro Cuore of Milan (CeTIF), AIS and Trento University.

The same software was used in another EC-financed project, again as a part of Esprit. In this project it is used to carry out behaviour analyses on Banca Monte dei Paschi s.p.a.'s customers, in order to spot potential clusters of customers interested in savings management. The other partners, besides the bank, are Southampton University's Parallel Applications Centre, were CeTIF of Milan's Catholic University and AIS.

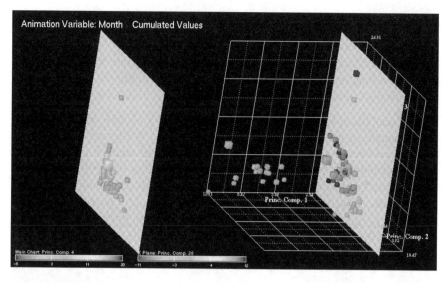

Figure 5.3   Visual analysis: anomaly search

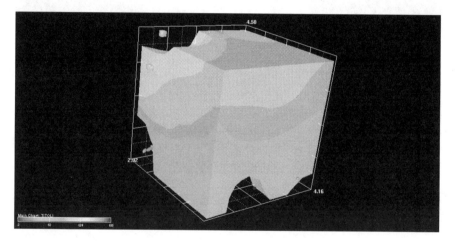

Figure 5.4   Visual analysis: behaviour of customers toward certain products and services.
Source: DBInspector

5.4   Neural Networks

Neural networks are among the most popular data mining techniques available. Through learning from a collection of historical data called a *learning set*, they are able to generate patterns and then validate them over another subset called the *test set*. They operate in an iterative way, continually modifying found patterns until they reach the optimum solution. They are also capable of previews over historical series as well as event classification (Taylor, 1911; Valino, Rubio, Villaverde, 1989).

Many applications thereof are to be found in the financial industry (Deboeck, 1995; Nottola, Rossignoli, 1995; Stein, 1991; Tarun, 1990; Turban, Trippi, 1993; Unwin, Cogbill, 1991).[21] They can be summarized as follows:

1. Screening over loan grants,

2. Evaluation of credit risk of mortgage loans,

3. Economic and financial forecasts,

4. Diversification and portfolio selection,

5. Simulation of market trends,

6. Customer segmentation,

7. Creation of profitability indexes,

8. Fraud detection,

9. Stock market trends forecasts,

10. Career planning and management.

5.4.1   Neural Networks: A Definition

The term "neural networks" identifies an intelligent processing technology that is complementary to traditional information technology (Tarun, 1990).

Given its extraordinary performances in calculation and problem solving, the human brain is the reference model for intelligent applications.

The human brain is made up of about 10 billion nerve cells called neurons, communicating through 1 million billion links called synapses. Activation of a neuron requires an electrical impulse to the other units it is linked to. By repetition of such an operation for each one of them, entire brain sections are activated within a few hundredths of second. However, the reader is referred to medicine and biology books for further information on the subject. A neuron is only 1/10 millionth as

---

[21] The same software was used in another EC-financed project, again as a part of Esprit. In this project it is used to carry out behaviour analyses on Banca Monte dei Paschi s.p.a.'s customers, in order to spot potential clusters of customers interested in savings management. The other partners beside the bank are Southampton University's Parallel Applications Centre, were CeTIF of Milan's Catholic University and AIS.

fast as a transistor; nevertheless, the human brain performs better than any computer. Neurologists reckon that its superiority originates from the great number of connections to each neuron. These ideas gave rise to the Neoconnectivist School (De Marco, 1988; Rossignoli, 1993).

While artificial intelligence scholars claim that it is possible to represent human knowledge using formal symbols and so to create programs that instruct a computer to make inferences by manipulation of these symbols, neoconnectivists do not agree with this view and do not believe that human thought is the product of interneural connections: therefore, they prefer to focus on interconnected networks. They maintain that the best way to find an answer is to let the system seek the solution by trying different connections until it finds the right one, rather than specifying a rule for the calculation (De Marco, 1988).

Therefore, a neural network is a set of techniques used for signal processing, previews and pattern recognition. If properly[22] implemented and trained they can be used to create complex and sophisticated statistical models, in order to obtain and analyse data relationships, foresee trends, or construct models that are valuable in terms of competitiveness and prediction. One of the many successful applications is in marketing (Dayhoff, 1990).

As in traditional information systems, neural networks consist of a set of input data, processing elements, and an output; the differences are in the processing, which is parallel and nonprocedural, and in the acquisition of knowledge, which is based exclusively on the input data.[23]

The structure of a neural network, as shown in Figure 5.5, is made up of several layers. The input layer contains n neurons, n being equal to the number of network inputs. The hidden layer, which can be single or multiple, includes n neurons, where n is not definable a priori. The output layer embodies n neurons, where n is equal to the number of desired outputs.

In the back-propagation networks each neuron in the input layer is linked to all the neurons in the hidden layer, and each neuron of this latter is linked to each neuron in the output layer.

---

[22] In terms of both good construction and integration with other technologies.

[23] This characteristic sets them apart from expert systems: as a matter of fact, in the latter the knowledge base has to be defined and inserted by an expert, while in neural networks knowledge acquisition comes from an auto-learning process based on historical data.

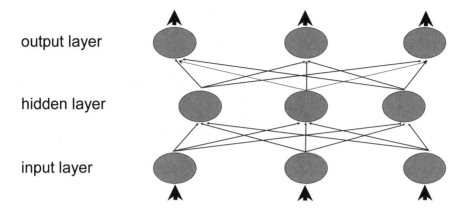

output layer

hidden layer

input layer

Figure 5.5   Structure of a neural network

A neuron receives a signal from the connections that link it to other neurons: it then combines the exciting and inhibiting signals it receives and sends a further signal that spreads as soon as global stimulation passes a certain threshold.

Figure 5.6 shows a single neuron's structure and its unidirectional connections to the subsequent layers (Wassermann, 1990); each connection is assigned a certain weighting, which varies according to the type of link existing between units. An element of the neural network receives a number of inputs from other elements and combines the values of it through particular processing (usually through a weighted sum). The outcome is modified by a transfer function, which can be a threshold function; otherwise, the output is generated if the sum passes a certain threshold, or a continuous function (Dayhoff, 1990). The value obtained is the output originating from the neuron, which could either constitute the input for a neuron of the subsequent layer, or an output if the neuron is an output neuron.

The neural network, through a self-learning process applied to input historical data considered relevant to the problem, is also able to perform previews on nonlinear problems, in other words the estimate of an output function. In the learning set phase the network adjusts, through an iterative procedure which modifies weights, the network outputs with the historical data, until it reaches the optimum point, where discrepancies between preview values, network outputs and historical values are at their smallest.

The subsequent phase, the test set, is aimed at evaluating the conformity of the output data provided by the network over a series of historical data which were not considered in the learning set phase.

Obviously, the output results are heavily influenced not only by the chosen input variables but also by a number of network configuration factors, such as, primar-

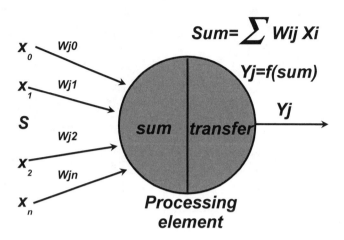

Figure 5.6   The structure of a neuron

ily, the network's structure and particularly the number of hidden layers which influence both network results and learning time. As a matter of fact, a network

with an excessive amount of hidden neurons and a high number of intermediate layers is bound to prolong learning time, without even enhancing output results. It could even provoke a loop (when the learning phase carries on without producing a satisfactory output, and the output does not improve with the learning time). In contrast, a network with a limited number of hidden neurons could lead to a poor learning level of the analysis undertaken (the classic example is the one where no intermediate layers exist, so that the network structure has just two levels, input and output, so that the estimated function is bound to be a linear one).

Secondarily, output results are affected by network configuration parameters, which influence the network's training and test processes. Among them are:

- The *learning rate,* which modifies the size of the corrections applied to the neurons' weight adjustment during the training phase. A value close to *1* allows quick learning. In many cases it could lead to an output.

- The momentum, which influences weight adjusting in the subsequent learning cycles: the closer the value is to 1 the more the weight adjustment affects the next learning process.

- The input noise, which allows for a certain noise tolerance in the network, such as the ability to work with uncertain, incomplete, and/or incorrect data, ranging from nil to 100%.

- Training and testing tolerance, which define the allowed error rate in the network output-historical data comparison phase, both in the training set phase and in the test set phase.

- The learning steps update and training cut-offs.

The third source of influence is the *enhanced parameters,* which allow for the choice of output function, connection weights, and adaptive learning rate.

The optimum combination of all these parameters, including the correct input factors, creates a network that is able to produce an output very close to the desired value; however, there is no rule to define a perfect combination a priori: it will take several trials to achieve a correct definition.

5.5   Genetic Algorithms

In the last few years, there has been a lot of interest in genetic algorithms[24] (Holland, 1975), whose starting point is the observation of natural phenomena. As a matter of fact, the inspiration for them came from Darwin's theory for the definition of computational paradigms aiming to solve complex problems.

Holland's conjectures are based on the following issues: (a) As in nature, genetic algorithms generate a better chromosome population each time by manipulating the previous generation. (b) As in nature, the algorithms have no knowledge of the final problem they have to solve. (c) The only information they have is an evaluation of the *fitness* of each chromosome in the population: the algorithms use this evaluation to allow reproduction to *fit* chromosomes and inhibit the ones with the worst rates (Holland, 1984).

This attention to natural algorithms owes the ability to solve problems in the same way as nature does to the scheme of transferring to calculation plots: indeed, the intention is to transpose living species' environment adaptation mechanisms into usable algorithms. Neural networks are the best example of the attempt to transfer the abilities of the human brain into an artificial system inspired by nature (Rumhelhart, 1986). Another example of a natural algorithm used to solve optimization problems is that of simulated annealing (the cooling process of a metal; Kirkpatrick, 1983). However, these examples are not the only ones used in information technology to solve optimization problems. In fact, other phenomena are observed, such as the evolution of species, the mutation and selection processes proposed by Darwin, the immune system, the organizational structure and problem-solving ability of ant colonies: they are all transferred to systems that simulate the same behaviours in the hope of finding the inspiration to design the same algorithms.

---

[24] John Holland was the one who initially proposed them.

Genetic algorithms differ from traditional optimization and procedure search methods in four main ways: they operate coding of a series of parameters, they carry out their research on a data population rather than on a single piece of information, they use a payoff information (objective function) rather than learning-originated knowledge, and they use probabilistic rules rather than deterministic ones (Holland, 1993).

5.5.1   A Definition of Genetic Algorithms

Genetic algorithms are parallel research algorithms used to solve optimization problems.

They are based on natural selection and genetic variation mechanisms (Goldberg, 1986). The calculation model takes its cue from the population genetics metaphor. The search for the final solution, as an optimization problem, is carried out through a proper balance of the need to explore new regions for the amount of available solutions, and the need to exploit, through a local search, the information already available, by analogy with population genetics. Each solution is considered individual, and the sum of all solutions for each time interval (t) is called the population (Holland, 1987).

The algorithms perform a simple cycle, composed of: population creation, reproduction and chromosome modification, and evaluation (Fig. 5.7).

In each generation, and according to the genetic diversity of its individuals' genetic heritage, pairs of individuals mate and create new individuals, whose genetic wealth is a combination of both parents' patrimonies. The adaptation of the individuals to the environment – the *fitness* – depends on their genetic heritage; hence, the fitter individuals are ahead and can live longer and in better health and reproduce more often, with the aim of transmitting to their offspring their competitive genetic features.

The genetic operators characterizing an algorithm are: crossover, substitution, mutation and inversion.

The crossover operator, which is the most frequently used, is applied with a probability independent of the individuals it is used for: it chooses two highly fit individuals and combines them to generate two offsprings that will have some of the first parent's chromosomes and some of the second one's. An example will clarify things:

1st parent   1 2 3 4 5 6;   2nd parent   7 8 9 10 11 12

a random cut is then carried out, e.g. in position 2, so that the result will be:

1° son   1 2 9 10 11 12   2° son   7 8 3 4 5 6

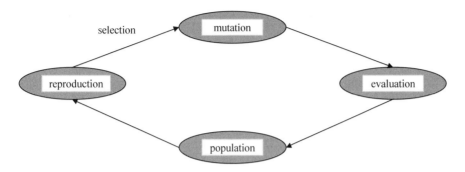

Figure 5.7   Genetic algorithms cycle

According to the above example, the offsprings result from the combination of both parents, and their chromosomes result from a random cut operated on the first and the second parent.

Since the other operators are less frequently used, it is not deemed necessary to show examples of their application.

5.5.2   Applications in Business and Financial Industry

Applications in this field have been growing steadily. The most relevant is the one carried out by Arthur, Holland, Palmer and Tayler (1991) at the Santa Fe Institute, which concerns a classifier system (machine learning systems using genetic algorithms). In this project, the classifier system is used as an artificial trader in order to learn about stock exchange dynamics. The classifier's objective was to learn, so as to find the best possible way to make a profit on investing a given sum of money. Its rules were set in random mode, and after 1000 generations they managed to form a set of behaviour rules for the artificial stock market. They created rules on how to buy when the price earnings multiple is low, and also simpler rules concerning the trend's perpetuation.

What is interesting about this application is that the classifier produced rules which not only created market-originated evaluation mechanisms, such as evaluations and mobile averages, but also elaborated rules on contemplating the other artificial traders' behaviour, so as to anticipate their moves. The rules provide interpretation for a number of currently used technical analysis methods, thus justifying their extensive use.

Another important observation was that the markets were steadily evolving, so that trading rules were short lived and had to be constantly adapted to the market's ever-changing situation (Arthur, Holland, Palmer, Tayler, 1991).

Another relevant application for genetic algorithms, which have aroused great interest among banks and financial institutions, is the one for customer behaviour. As a matter of fact, forecast models could help banks, insurance companies and stockbrokers to select the customers to whom they should send information about new products, customers with the lowest risk rate, and customers whose accounts could lead to further business opportunities.

The forecast system described above is the FUGA – Financial Utility using Genetic Algorithms – (Barrow, 1992), which is aimed at producing forecast systems more powerful than the ones obtained with traditional techniques for forecasting credit and insurance risk and at allowing simple and quick implementation of decision models that can be used by persons with no technical background, such as credit and marketing managers. FUGA is constructed by way of a wider spectrum forecast tool called GAAF[25] (Genetic Algorithm for the Approximation of Formulae).

Genetic algorithms may be rewardingly implemented in connection with other types of systems. A widely used integration is that with neural networks: the historical data used by the neural network can be "refined" by genetic applications, in order to obtain a better network output. The optimization process is a phase of selection and re-elaboration of the data aimed at selecting the most relevant and fittest ones and organizing them, in order to prepare a more efficient set of variables. This in turn will allow for a shorter response time, a better selection of relevant input data, and the choice of the best possible time interval.

Genetic algorithms are also associated with neural networks to optimize configuration factors such as parameters (learning rate, momentum and initial weight), type of activation function (linear, gaussian, etc.), learning criteria (pattern selection etc.), architecture (number of hidden layers and neurons), type of network (back propagation, recurring networks, Kohonen networks, etc.), and method of data choice for the test set (Deboeck, 1995). Algorithms manage to estimate the best combination of the above factors, eliminating the ones with fewer chances of success and thus obtaining the best configuration, the fittest one, and the one that will produce the best network output.

Further integration opportunities lie in the concurrent use of expert systems, neural networks, genetic algorithms, fuzzy logic, case-based reasoning, and machine learning, which leads to the so-called hybrid systems.

---

[25] GAAF was developed within the ESPRIT III – PAPAGENA project, which was sponsored by the EU.

5.6 Fuzzy Logic

Fuzzy logic systems derive from the graduated sets theory and go back to the studies on undefined value logic (Dubois, Prada, 1980). Fuzzy systems are meant to implement, in the decision process, mechanisms able to manage information characterized by qualitative elements or a low decision grade. One of fuzzy logic's principal functions is the definition of the sphere in which decision processes are to take place, especially as the program interacts with the outside world (Rossignoli, 1997).

Therefore, fuzzy logic is often considered a flexible tool through which a system can at the same time receive instructions and give the user explanations on activities carried out (Kingdon, Feldman, 1995).

The main advantage of fuzzy logic is that products based on it are less expensive and more precise than products based on classic logic control.

Fuzzy logic is closer to the real world and to the common way of thinking; this is one of the reasons why it is largely implemented in association with neural networks (Kosko, 1992). Its force lies precisely in its ability to grasp the subtleties of the physical world. In contrast, classic logic divides the world into sharply defined classes, losing all nuances in the process. All this reflects on fuzzy logic's practical applications, the first examples of which go back to the beginning of the 1990s, when several fuzzy-based devices were created (Kosko, 1996).

As a consequence of fuzzy logic, fuzzy systems have been created. Being a practical application of fuzzy logic, they are the most recent result of this discipline and may be considered as "universal function approximators": in other words, they can simulate the course of functions, even strongly nonlinear ones, through a number of fuzzy rules sets and without using mathematic formulas.

The most common criticism of fuzzy logic is that it supposedly does not add anything to statistical theories. Such activities can just be done using the other theories.

Actually, fuzzy logic is very different from the probability theory. The misunderstanding is due to the fact that both describe uncertainty using numbers included between 0 and 1. Still, the uncertainties described are different in the two theories. The fuzzy theory describes the ambiguity of events, namely to what degree an event takes place, and not whether an event takes place or not, which is what the probability theory describes.

Contingent fallbacks in the development of the fuzzy theory in the information technology field would be due precisely to the ease of implementing neural networks through computers, thus providing useful tools for the design of fuzzy systems (Kosko, 1992).

One of the possible applications in the finance industry is the evaluation of the weight of a qualitative variable on the stock market trend. If the aim is to attribute a quantitative and objective value – leaving aside all subjective considerations – to a political event liable to condition the stocks trend, it can be done using a fuzzy logic system: for it is able to parameterize, so to speak, a qualitative variable and turn it into a quantitative and objective one.

They can also be successfully employed to improve understanding of customer profiles in CRM activities.

5.7   Rule Induction and Decision Trees

Rule induction and decision trees are models operating as follows: they divide the data subset into smaller sets, each of which is explained by a number of rules. The output of such systems allows automatic identification of rules and models through learning from historical data. Once spotted, rules and models can be used to analyse new data subsets. The advantage lies in the fact that the user is able to identify and analyse the rules found out by the system; however, the drawback is that the system often produces a great many rules which can be hard to interpret and manage.

5.7.1   Rule Induction

Rule induction is a technique that allows data relationships to be spotted and expressed in the form of rules. The starting point is a set of historical examples, each having a number of features and belonging to a different class. Through subsequent inferences, the system finds out the characteristics common to each class, trying to extrapolate the rules that define them through the smallest possible number of conditions. The results obtained can then be used to classify new sets of examples.

This technique divides the data subset in smaller sets, each of which is explained by a number of rules. The output of such sets allows automatic identification of rules and models through learning from historical data. The system subsequently extracts the rules from the database and visualizes them for the user, arranging them according to their frequency and to the number of times they have proven right. Once identified, rules or models may be used to analyse new data subsets.

The advantage, compared with other approaches, is that the user, however unfamiliar with the application domain, is able to identify and analyse the rules that were spotted by the system. The drawback of it is that often a great many rules are produced, which can be hard to interpret and manage.

5.7.2   Decision Trees

Decision trees are forecast models designed to select the variables that are best to explain the target's variability through subdivision of the data set analysed. A feature peculiar to this method is the immediate interpretation of results: the graphic representation of the tree shows internal data relationships in a simple and intuitive way, thus making analysis results evident. However, decision trees have a tendency to overgrow, making interpretation difficult in actual applications, since the number of attributes and the values they can acquire are often remarkable. To overcome this inconvenience some alternatives have been studied, e.g. division of the original tree into a hierarchy of subtrees. Decision trees are successfully implemented in supervised learning systems to classify objects in a given number of classes. The tree's nodes are labelled with the attributes' names; the branches show the various values that the attributes can have (the conditions that determined the subdivision); and the leaves represent the classes (data set partitions). According to the type of partition, we speak of binary (two-way partitions are used, see Fig. 5.8), ternary (three), or multiple (several) clustering.

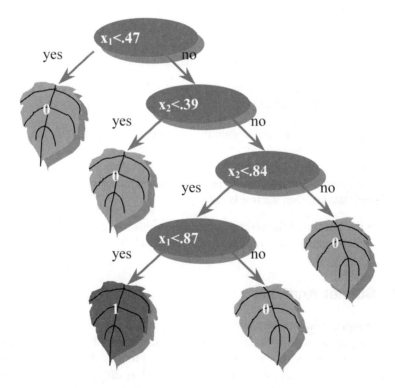

Figure 5.8   Decision trees and binary data clustering

To classify a case, we have to start from the root and progress through the nodes and down to the leaves. It may be remarked that decision trees are suitable for the analysis of data both qualitative and quantitative in nature.

The algorithms most frequently used in the construction of a decision tree are:

- C4.5 (improved version of the ID3 algorithm introduced at the end of the 1970s by J.R. Quinlan),

- CART, standing for Classification and Regressing Trees (Breiman, Friedman, Olshen, Stone, 1984),

- CHAID (Chi-square Automatic Interaction Detector).

In order to decide when to stop the partition process, several methods are used, although the optimum is to use them all concurrently. (Del Ciello, Dulli, Saccardi, 2000). The most frequently used are:

- Maximum number of steps in the process,

- Minimum size of groups,

- Minimum deviance of the parent group,

- Minimum explaining capacity of the best subdivision at every step,

- Pruning (which is not an interruption rule but a procedure designed to decrease the tree's size by cutting off the less significant branches).

A relevant factor is the tree's stability. A way to establish it is the random substitution of some data, in order to observe the differences from the original data set. Another method is the subdivision of the data set in several random parts and the confrontation of the results obtained. If these are the same in both cases, as in the original data set, then the tree is stable.

Decision trees are used for several applications, either to explore data and create (for example) segmentation, or to create forecast models.

5.8   Cluster Analysis

The techniques that obtain classification plots dividing a population into sub-groups include clustering. Given a number of statistical units, for which a certain number of variables is known, cluster analysis aims to seek disjointed subsystems that are as homogeneous as possible internally and as different as possible from one another, compared with the input variables (Berry, Linoff, 1997).

Table 5.1   Advantages and drawbacks of the most popular data mining systems

TECHNIQUES	ADVANTAGES	DRAWBACKS
Visualization	The user can visualize large amounts of data, discover relationships and test them	Requires a statistical expert who is also able to use other data mining techniques
Neural networks	High elaboration capability as for data with nonlinear relationships. Ability to work with incomplete and "noisy" data	Inability to explain results obtained, although it is possible to use other systems for the interpretation. Qualitative data have to be turned into quantitative ones
Genetic algorithms	Good forecast capacity using data concealing nonlinear relationships	Inability to explain results obtained, although it is possible to use other systems for the interpretation. Qualitative data have to be turned into quantitative ones
Fuzzy logic	Ability to classify variables and results according to proximity to desired solution	Limited number of providers and applications available on the market
Rule induction and decision tree	Creation of rules and models based on historical data. Rules and models are plain to see and easy to interpret	They require fine-tuning in order to avoid overproduction of figures and rules, which would be difficult to interpret and manage

The phrase "cluster analysis" is often, and erroneously, used as a synonym of, or in association with, segmentation techniques. The latter actually refer to the identification of groups with mutual characteristics through segmentation of the information amount in previously defined groups; clustering aims to segment data into classes that are not yet decided, identified or defined, that is to say without knowing a priori the distinctive features of each class or the total number of them. Within this category, it is possible to comprise Kohonen's self-organizing maps or networks. In the same way, some authors (Edelstein, 2000) include, not entirely wrongly, fuzzy algorithms in the clustering techniques: these too are discussed separately in a dedicated paragraph.

As previously pointed out, when groups are formed, attempts are made to maximize internal homogeneity while at the same time emphasizing the differences between groups. In order to find out which statistical units belong to which group distances are calculated, which implies the choice of an adequate measuring unit, with the aim of expressing at best the distances between the sample elements that are to be examined. In short, the analysis input is a quantitative data matrix, carrying for each statistical unit the value of the variables upon which the classification is to be made, while the output is a new categorical variable with modes representing the group to which each statistical unit is unerringly assigned.

There are two main classes of classification algorithms:

- The hierarchical algorithms: each group belongs to a bigger one. In their turn, they can be subdivided into: cleaving algorithms, where for X units we have X groups, as the clusters obtained are, step by step, subsets of a group formed at the previous stage, so that at the end each group includes a single unit; aggregating algorithms, which work by a logic that is exactly the reverse of the above.

- As for the nonhierarchical algorithms, the necessary input parameter is the number of clusters to be obtained and the primary values (centroids[26]) of them. The algorithm, through an iterative process and according to the assigned number of classes, tries to achieve the best classification of the statistical units. At each odd step, the closest groups are put together, while at every even step the most inhomogeneous cluster is separated OUT; the computation of the centroids carries on until their drifting from one step to the next becomes infinitesimal. Here as well, two categories can be found: partitioned algorithms, generating classes which exclude one another and superimposed ones, which admit the possibility of an entity belonging to more than one class.

Among the fundamental steps needed for a cluster analysis to be carried out on a set of variables, three phases deserve particular mention: identification of the variables to be classified, selection of the proximity measure between variables, and selection of the classification algorithm.

In short, given the data matrix object of the analysis, it is necessary to insert the variables observed or an adequate transformation of them in the analysis. It is often important to render the variables independent of the measure scale through appropriate standardization. When the number of variables is large, or when the aim is to eliminate redundancy, a convenient transformation is the application of factor analysis to the observed data, in order to turn them into something more suitable.

---

[26] The exact definition of centroid is „vector of the averages of a multi-varied distribution."

As for the second problem, the real starting point of the analysis is the measurement of the distance between the units to be classified. In order to do this, one of the following three statistical measure units is usually applied: the Euclidean distance, the average absolute distance, and the Lagrange–Tchebychev distance.

Concerning the choice of a classification algorithm, it is necessary to refer to the two main categories previously mentioned. Hierarchical algorithms do not require an a priori definition of the number of groups to be obtained, but are very demanding from a computational point of view, so that they should be avoided when the number of statistical units is large. Nonhierarchical algorithms appear to be very much more efficient, as they can manage data sets of great magnitude and are hardly influenced by anomalous values. What is more, not being monotonous, they can allow a statistical unit, initially belonging to a certain cluster, to switch groups during the iterative process.

In marketing analyses, and in marketing generally, these data mining classification methods are useful every time it is necessary to gather consumers, products, markets, areas, etc., into homogeneous classes. In particular, such techniques may be used to analyse consumer tastes, find the aggregate of competition goods, or trace product hierarchies. An implementation closer to CRM issues is their use to operate segmentation of the customer portfolio according to its behaviour (Berry, Linoff, 1997).

6 The Evolution of Customer Relationships and Customer Value

6.1 From a "Transactional" to a "Relational" Approach

Today's companies operate within a complex economic environment featuring continuous and radical changes owing to the steady arrival of new kinds of competition.

Many factors push companies in the direction of change, including the market and the development of new technologies (Groenroos, 1990). First, customers are getting more and more particular, declining standard products and services and attentive to the available alternatives. Purchase choices are value-for-money oriented as much as they are influenced by the search for personalized products able to fulfil individual requirements. Second, if technology evolution allows companies to provide new products and services more easily, it forces them at the same time to look for new strategies in order to differentiate themselves from the competition.

Hence the need to turn away from the transactional approach, which is focused on short-term-oriented (McDonald, Rogers, 1999) single sales and on the product's features, with scarce and discontinuous contacts with customers. From the transactional perspective, the relationship between company and customers is conflictual in nature and limited to the negotiation (quantity, price, delivery terms etc.) and service provision phases.

Therefore, companies have to adapt a relational approach, that is to say a strategy meant to develop and reinforce steady and durable relationships with customers, who become active partners in the process of innovating and creating value (Figure 6.1).

This different vision of the market makes abandonment of the traditional concepts of marketing management inevitable and contributes to the development of so-called interactive or relational marketing.

According to Berry (1983), "marketing is the establishment, maintenance and reinforcement (usually, though not always, on a long term basis) of relationships with customers and other partners, in order to achieve the objectives of all the parties involved. This is obtainable through a reciprocal exchange and a mutual keeping of promises."

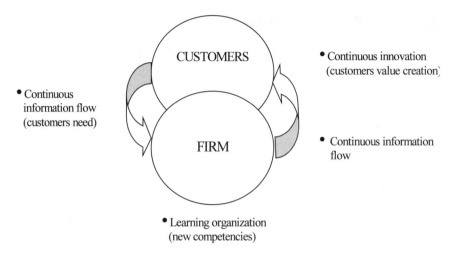

Figure 6.1   Value loop. Source: Cantone, 1996

The market is regarded more as a network of stable relationships between a number of actors (customers, companies, providers and competitors) than just as a combination of exchanges. The single transaction is no longer the key to economic activities, as it becomes part of a steady relational process, which in turn creates a system of exchanges.

All organizations are striving to become more and more customer centred: in order to acquire, increase or maintain a competitive advantage, they have to set the customer and customer satisfaction at the centre of most of the company's choices and decisions (Cuomo, 2000).

All resources, including personnel, technology and systems, must be used to preserve and increase the customer's fidelity to the company.

The adaptation of this kind of approach requires sharing of information, technological and management know-how, so as to imply a radical change in company vision and business processes, starting from the company culture, right through all organizational structures, systems, and management and operational processes.

6.2   The Company Culture

In order to create value within the company it is necessary to diffuse an overall system of shared values and rules, which lead each member to behave in such a way as to meet customers' expectations through the range of offered services.

A further requirement is the establishment of a climate of cohesion between all the phases and functions of the process (so-called interfunctional collaboration), which allows achievement of the ultimate goal, customer satisfaction.

This last, in fact, now has to be considered a resource, a business value that should be cherished in order to gain a relevant position in the realm of potential demand.

To maintain and reinforce its customer relationship and competitive market position, the company has to keep a constant focus on the increase in the supplied value.

The sharing of the value culture is possible only if the concepts of value and customer orientation are explicitly stressed in the company's mission and strategy statement. The diffusion of a customer-oriented culture, especially within sizeable companies, is often a difficult task. If the structure is consolidated and existing values do not reflect customer priority, there should be a cautious intervention aiming to overcome the force of habit and resistance to change. Naturally, the more widespread and the more firmly rooted the old values are, the harder it will be and the longer it will take to defeat them (Cantone, 1996).

The spreading process may take place through either a *top-down* or a *bottom-up* approach (Cuomo, 2000). In the former, the company management revisits the fundamental principles of the company culture and tries to spread them throughout the underlying hierarchical levels. In the latter, in contrast, the inputs are acquired at the base of the hierarchical pyramid through continuous contacts with outside and are diffused within the organization via ascending mechanisms. This last method appears to be the more suitable to create a customer-driven approach.

6.3   The Organizational Structure

Perrone (1990) defines organizational structure as "the result of the choices through which work is divided and coordinated within an organized system."

It is possible to identify both a "horizontal dimension", meaning the division of work and the functional specialization, and a "vertical dimension" defining hierarchical relationships between all subjects and organs involved in decision and operative processes (Perrone, 1990, Decastri, 1984; Drucker 1973).

The way the organizational structure is designed affects the performing mode of all company activities: those creating value within the company and those relating to interaction with customers and providers.

The traditional company structure is represented as a multilayer pyramid with a peak, a number of intermediate levels, and a base in contact with the market. At the top is top management, which takes all the decisions about whatever activities are to be carried out. One step below we find the middle management, which converts the decisions into instructions, rules, policies and orders, and transmits them down the line (Fontana, 1995; Carlzon, 1991).

The base contains the *front-line* personnel, persons who are in regular contact with customers yet have none of the decisional power necessary to face the problems that constantly come up (Carlzon, 1991).

In a customer-oriented company the role distribution is different, for in this environment flatter and more nearly horizontal structures come to life, with authority and responsibility transferred from the management to the front line. This is called an "upside-down pyramid" (Fig. 6.2). According to this configuration, the front-line staff stand at the top of the organization, and the front line includes all personnel, physical resources and operative systems that interact directly with the customers. This level bears the responsibility for responding promptly and courteously to the customers' specific problems, so as to achieve the best possible perception of service quality.

In order to do this, both middle and top management operate with the creation of value for customers in mind: analysis of problems, effective resource allocation,

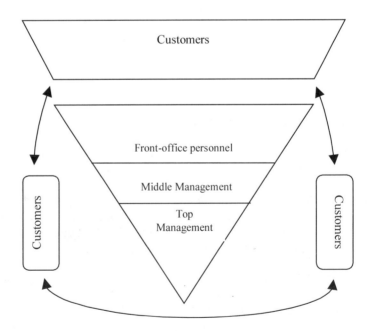

Figure 6.2   Upside-down pyramid. Source: adapted by Carlzon, 1991

and provision of all the support necessary to the front-line workers to enable them to behave in an adequate manner when facing the "moments of truth" defined by Groenroos (1990) as "the interactions between the customers' representatives and the various company resources."

6.4   The Main Processes of Organizations

The main processes include all systems concerned in the direction of planning and control, of information, communication, and human resource organization.

Configuration and management of the above processes are the fundamental tools in spreading the customer orientation culture at every company level. A determinant role is played by the human resources, because the personnel is directly involved in maximizing the value created and provided. Front-line operators, being in direct contact with customers, are in a position to perceive external signals and current trends, making it possible for the company to manage them in due course.

New methods are studied and implemented by means of strong investments in training and personnel development programmes, so as to give employees direct responsibilities in decision processes and policies directed at increasing value for customer. This kind of involvement is required in order to enhance personnel "faith" in the organization, which in turn leads to quality improvement in products/services provided, cost reduction, higher profitability and customer fidelization (Currie, Galliers, 1999).

Equally important is the role of information technology. The introduction of hardware and software systems capable of quick gathering, elaboration and transmission of information and knowledge can enhance both operational efficiency (leading to a cost reduction) and value production for the customer (Galliers, Baets, 2000).

As a matter of fact, it is possible to achieve:

- Integration of the company with its customers,
- Better knowledge of market and demand,
- More articulated market segmentation, leading to an improved ability of the company to
  - Forecast changes in market requirements and expectations,
  - Design a supply system able to respond quickly and adequately to demand requirements,
  - Differentiate from competitors.

We refer to the use of point-of-sale scanners (POS), which in retail distribution companies allow a number of evaluations, e.g. the consistency of the product range with the reference target, or the effectiveness of marketing and advertising activities.

Another interesting feature is the use of marketing databases or datamarts, which can provide detailed information on customers and on their purchasing behaviour, which is useful to operate an efficient segmentation and to plan especially aimed strategies for each customer class.

Last but not least, intranet/extranet networks permit real-time sharing of vast amounts of information among users.

6.5   Who is the Customer?

According to the *customer value-based* approach, the company's main task is to create value in favour of all the interest groups it has contact with, all of whose members, in a broader sense, can be considered customers.

It is possible to distinguish between external and internal customers: the former being the ultimate and intermediate customers (so-called industrial users), commercial brokers, and all other subjects the company establishes partnerships or collaboration agreements with, while the latter are stock holders, managers, employees, etc.

Fulfilment of their expectations is essential to the achievement of the company's general objectives.

The company creates value for the interest groups when it is able to determine the greatest possible positive spread between the costs and benefits perceived by these subjects while they are interacting with it.

This is called perceived use value (PUV) (Cantone, 1996), meaning the value the customer believes he has acquired as soon as he is able to put the purchased product/service to use:

$$PUV = Pb - Pc$$

where:

Pb = perceived benefits

Pc = perceived costs for effort, resulting from the sum of monetary and opportunity costs (waiting time, physical effort, disservices) sustained during the purchase process.

In order to plan initiatives likely to influence the customer's decisions and perceptions, the company has to be able to detect the perceived offer quality, the way comparisons with the competition are carried out, and the way the target market operates its purchase choices (Brown, 2000; Burnett, 2001).

To obtain this kind of information, however, it is necessary previously to have assessed who the company's customers are by means of market segmentation, a tool that is fundamental to the search of competitive advantages (Stone, Woodcock, Machtynger, 2000).

For segmentation to be useful, the segments must have certain well-defined characteristics (Kotler, Scott, 1997), which are:

a) Measurability – size and buying power of each segment have to be measurable.

b) Accessibility – it must be possible to actually reach and serve the segments.

c) Importance – segments must be wide and absorbent enough to be profitable.

d) Practicability – the company must be able to implement programmes and strategies necessary to attract and serve the chosen segments.

We may begin by tracing a "market map" showing the odd purchase mechanisms present in the market, and also the value chain, which involves all actors, from the provider to the final user.

Then we proceed with the description and features analysis of the customer groups spotted. Several classes of variables influencing purchase behaviour are taken into account: socio-demographic (e.g. geographic areas, age, sex, and income), psychographic (e.g. social class, lifestyle, and personality), and behaviour-related variables (e.g. product use, expected benefits, consume rate).

Next comes the analysis of all relevant competitive products/services, along with the respective distribution channels.

In fact, the more the company knows about market structure and dynamics, the better it can focus its efforts on the more promising opportunities, in order to offer better value to its customers (Ciborra, 2000; Brown, 2000; Berson, Smith, Thearling, 2000).

6.5.1   The Relationship with Internal Customers

The phrase "internal customers" identifies the array of company organizational units (functions, sections, offices) that receive products and services from other units or from outside in order to carry out their particular activities (in short, all the employees of the company). Each internal customer is both customer and provider toward the other units and outside, respectively. This implies the development of constant interactions and relationships, which constitute the "inner customer chain" (Cantone, 1996; Rajola, 1999). Its prerequisites are:

- Organization and management per processes,

- Interfunctional integration,

- Teamwork.

Management and optimization of the inner customer chain are issues that are of fundamental importance to the company, for, after all, external customer satisfaction depends on inner customer performance. The company must be able to control personnel behaviour and internal communication. Only in this way can it manage to:

- Enhance the efficiency and effectiveness of company activities,

- Promote interfunctional integration as the critical factor for the development of new products and processes,

- Increase personnel motivation and satisfaction, involving it directly in problem solving,

- Spread a customer-oriented company culture, where every member gets to be an internal marketer, in order to maximize the value he/she produces within the process he/she belongs to.

It is possible to represent the process graphically through a stylized spiral (Figure 6.3): the increase in value produced per outer customer generates satisfaction and gratification for the personnel who have contributed to it, thus reinforcing common values and objectives, sense of belonging, and loyalty.

6.5.2   The Relationship with Outer Customers

This relationship can be classified over a matrix obtained by crossing the variables "community of goals" and "value of relationship" as perceived by the provider. Four types of relationship are identified (Cantone, 1996):

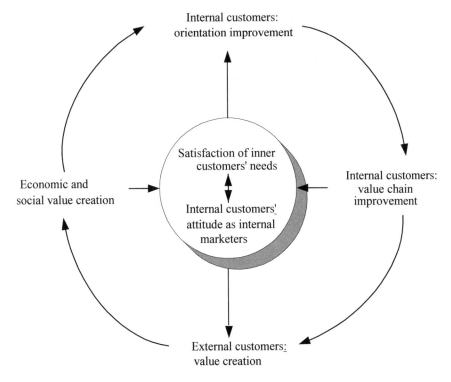

Figure 6.3   Satisfaction of internal customers' needs as value creation for external customers. Source: Cantone, 1996

- *Partners*: High relationship value and high communality in objectives. These are long-term, exclusive relationships, in which both parts take an active role in the value-creating process.

- *Friends*: Low relationship value, high goal community.

- *Rivals*: High relationship value, but low goal communality. It is a short-term, conflicting, opportunistic relationship.

- *Acquaintances*: Low relationship value and low goal communality. The relationship is based on a short-term, opportunistic logic, each part seeking to exploit its own exclusive advantages.

As already stated, the establishment of a durable relationship with customers is a critical factor in a company's success. Two are the principles that lead the companies toward this objective especially in business-to-business markets. They are (Stone, Woodcock, Machtynger, 2000; Cantone, 1996; Gilmore, Pine, 2000; Burnett, 2001):

- The satisfaction of customers' expectations, by proposing offers that come increasingly close to the customers' ever-changing needs,

- The involvement of customers in the value-creation process, through stable and coordinated relationships, allowing recognition of which aspects, material or immaterial, of the offer need to be changed in order to maintain and possibly improve the company's competitiveness (Berson, Smith, Thearling, 2000).

The relationship must be based on the communality of goals; company and customers have to collaborate to share the benefits that emerge.

As a matter of fact, the following advantages derive from the adaptation of a relational approach (Stone, Woodcock, Machtynger, 2000; Cantone, 1996):

- A deep knowledge of the factors and preferences that pilot the customers' purchase choices,

- Containment of costs and problems related to the definition and development of the product/service,

- Capitalization of consumer experience,

- Ability to forecast a change in the customers' needs,

- Reduction of uncertainty and lowering of market and technological risks,

- Development of mutual faith and loyalty,

- Enhanced service quality, in both quality and efficiency,

- Vast possibilities in offer personalization.

6.6   The Customer's Life Cycle

Each company–customer interaction is part of a deeper relationship, which has several development stages. Therefore, it might be useful to consider a temporal evolution horizon, during which the providing company will carry out a number of initiatives, in order to promote the development of the relationship and thus fully exploit the customer's purchase potential (Nadin, 2000).

At the origin of what we may call the "customer relationship life cycle" is the potential customer (Fig: 6.4). He may not even be acquainted with the company and its products/services (Imhoff, Loftis, Geiger, Inmon, 2001; Keene, 2001). In this phase, the company's efforts are highly relevant, for it will try, through initiatives designed to attract attention (Nadin, Cerri, 1999), to get to know its potential customers and create interest in its offer.

When the customer realizes he has certain needs that might be met by a certain company we enter the interactivity phase, which ideally ends with a purchase.

During the purchase process (so-called adaptation phase) the potential customer evaluates the offered product with reference to both its ability to actually meet his needs and his inclination to pay for it (Blattberg, Getz, Thomas, 2001).

We then reach the consumption or use stage, in which the consumer establishes the functional and technical features of the good, as well as the company's ability to provide assistance and subsidiary services (Bielski, 2000).

If the customer is satisfied, the odds are that the relationship will continue, leading to new purchases; otherwise the customer can leave the path at any moment and contact the competition (Hall, 1999; Kiesnoski, 1999).

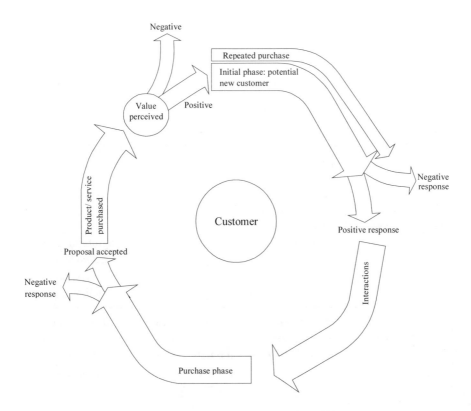

Figure 6.4   Customer relationship life cycle. Source: Nadin, 2000

In the case of business-to-business markets, the relationship may lead to the establishment of actual commercial partnerships.

The company should be able to recognize (Groenroos, 1990):

- In which phase of the cycle the customers it wants to reach are,

- What actions and initiatives are required at each phase (Table 6.1) to retain the largest possible number of customers.

Table 6.1   Objectives, strategies and initiatives of the company in each phase of the customer relationship life cycle (Source: Nadin, Cerri, 1999)

	OBJECTIVES	STRATEGY	INITIATIVES
ATTRACTING ATTENTION	Spot suspects Select prospects	Increase brand popularity	Introduce company and the products/services it has on offer
INTERACTIVITY	Anticipate needs and seek affinity	Draw interest in prospects	Evaluate customer needs Carry out test orders
ADAPTATION	Seek actual affinity	Ensure quality and satisfaction	Interact with the customer by personalizing the offer
REQUIREMENT	Loyalize the customer Increase penetration	Promote customer service	Cross selling Programming and management of purchases, orders, and deliveries
COMMERCIAL PARTNERSHIP	Develop both customer and provider business	Promote development initiatives through communal investments	Sign concession deals Joint design of new products

6.7   The Concepts of Customer Satisfaction and Loyalty

6.7.1   Definition and Role of Customer Satisfaction

Owing to the radical changes taking place in the company-market relationship, the satisfaction of the customers' needs is now a necessary condition of company survival.

There is no unanimous definition of customer satisfaction in the literature (Cuomo, 2000; Rajola, 1999); however, it is possible to identify three main orientations:

a) Psychocognitive: this school studies the motivations at the base of customer satisfaction, comparing expected benefits with actually obtained ones. When the former match the latter, we speak of *confirmation*, as opposed to *disconfirmation* in the case of discrepancies.

b) Operational: this one ties customer satisfaction to a number of actions and technical solutions, for which business units have direct contact with customers.

c) Strategic: the customer is regarded as a major factor in the company's survival and development. *Customer* satisfaction is viewed as a downright philosophy, "an entrepreneurial *modus operandi* explicating the ability to create value for customers, anticipating and managing their expectations and showing in all tactical choices competence and responsibility, in order to fulfil their needs."

The above are three different yet complementary approaches. As a matter of fact, it is not possible to implement a customer satisfaction system "operationally" without having in mind a strategic vision of the customer's satisfaction and without considering the psychocognitive aspects of the consumer's behaviour.

Now we have stressed the strategic importance of customer satisfaction, it is possible to analyse its role within the company's organizational approaches, for which we refer to three relational levels (Cuomo, 2000):

a) In the strictest sense, the customer-oriented approach is used only for final consumers.

b) In a wider sense, attention is focused on all subjects with any kind of relationship with the company (providers, competitors, personnel), since all operators, internal and external, are actually company customers.

c) In an integrated sense, customer strategies are applied collectively to all company partners within the same production area or strategic group, in order to gain competitive strength and increase each component's value.

The company's behaviour may not be unequivocal, but it will have to be consistent with the position it occupies at that given moment.

In any case, the company must be aware that the customer himself is the source of the strongest and most constructive inputs that allow it to take up a proactive role and give rise to a virtuous circle (Fig. 6.5), which will lead in time to substantial increases in competitive advantages (Valdani, 1995; Morris, 2002).

The company is only able to produce sustainable competitive advantages if its offer generates a positive or neutral differential between the perceived use value (PUV) (Cantone, 1996) and the expected value (EV) (Rountree, 2001; Pavia, 1999; Morris, 2002; Cantone, 1996):

$$S = PUV - EV$$

where:

S   = "absolute" customer satisfaction

EV = the net value the customer expects to obtain once the offered product/service is at his full disposal, which is given by the difference between expected benefits (EB) and expected costs (EC).

In order to compare the degree of satisfaction provided by the company's offer, as opposed to the one provided by the competition, it is necessary to refer to the "relative" or "comparative" satisfaction, i.e. the relation between the absolute satisfaction produced by the company and the average absolute satisfaction produced by all competitors.

The consumer is considered as the fundamental party to establish a durable relationship with, through the activation of bi-directional communication channels, allowing sharing of values and full appreciation of incoming information about the customers (Morris, 2002).

This can explain the statement that customer satisfaction affects both internal and external relationships. In fact, strong and steady interactions are created, based on objective sharing and on collaboration for the achievement of expected results.

The direct involvement contributes to the creation of a favourable climate, leading to an increase in the company's ability to create value, as well as to effectively anticipate and manage customers' expectations, be they internal or external.

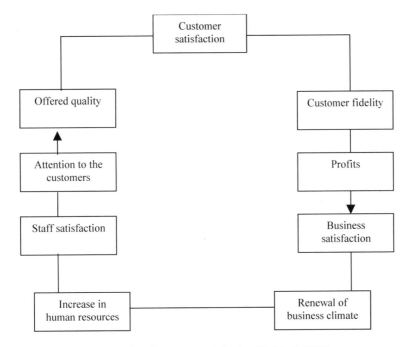

Figure 6.5   The virtuous circle of customer satisfaction (Valdani, 1995)

This virtuous circle allows the company to consolidate its strong points and improve its competitive advantage, even in the presence of an increasingly global and critical market. From this standpoint, customer satisfaction is the major asset for the creation of the conditions needed to loyalize customers (Keene, 2001).

6.7.2   Organizing the Concept of Loyalty

The 1990s have established the importance of customer satisfaction as the key element in the implementation of effective growth and power-up strategies (Nadin, 2000). A further objective has been added since, namely customer loyalty (Keene, 2001). As a matter of fact, satisfaction is a decisive factor in establishing a lasting relationship with the customer and gaining his loyalty, particularly for those firms which, not enjoying a dominant market position based on distinctive and unique competencies, have to face extremely lively competition and are liable to loss of even the customers they have already acquired (Nadin, 2000).

In the business-to-business area, it is often the customer who seeks a tight bond with his provider. This is especially true for network companies, which need strong partners to whom they can entrust nonvital, yet no less important, phases of their management processes (Ptacek, 2001).

But what, then, is loyalty exactly? Oliver (1997) has defined it as "a deep commitment to constantly reacquire or promote products or services, in spite of the influence of particular situations and competition marketing efforts, which could potentially affect the company's behaviour."

To put it simply, it is about defining the conditions that will cause the customer to stick to the same company in the future.

The loyalty creation process can ideally be subdivided into evolution phases (PricewaterhouseCoopers, 2000):

a) Knowledge phase: the company must get to know the customer and his expectations. Loyalty is virtually absent from this phase, for the relationship is merely based on the knowledge of products and prices. The customer might very well switch to a competitor boasting a better offer.

b) Emotional or understanding phase: the company watches and analyses the customer's behaviour in all phases leading up to and following the purchase. Loyalty is no longer based only on product and price, for the relationship between customer and provider is getting to be the key factor.

c) Will or loyalization phase: the relationship with the customer must become a personal one. In order to maintain and enhance loyalty, the satisfaction level must be high and reciprocal.

Therefore, loyalty is a primary objective for the achievement of lasting positive effects, even in the case of price modifications making the prices higher than the competition's (premium price). In fact, if the customer is loyal, he is likely to stick to his brand even if the competition is cheaper, for he will focus more on the value-for-money ratio than purely on the price. He will even be willing to purchase other products offered by the same company (cross-selling), thus contributing to a multiplication mechanism of sorts, based on the "bush telegraph" created by people expressing their satisfaction to each other.

While it is absurd to think of a company not having customer satisfaction among its objectives, it is certainly possible to find companies which prefer maintaining a high customer turnover rate to investing in loyalty (Nadin, 1999).

These situations are properly shown in the "decisional matrix" (Fig. 6.6). The matrix shows:

- Two completely antithetical situations (pure loyalization and spot exchange),

- One transition situation, typical of companies entering a new market or testing neighbouring businesses (eat and run),

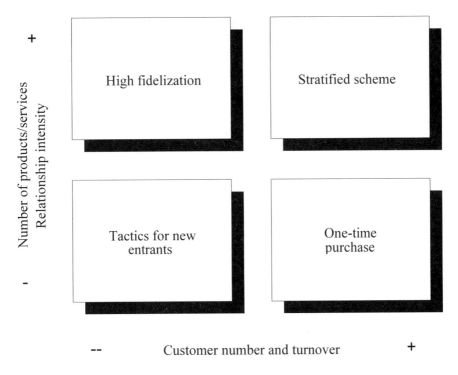

Figure 6.6   Decision matrix (Source: adapted by Nadin, 2000)

- A situation combining pure loyalization and a maximum market extension model (layered pattern).

Companies which decide not to focus on loyalization will not be able to fully exploit the potential given by a lasting relationship with the customer, and will therefore try to maintain a large number of customers and a quick turnover (which is the typical logic of companies operating in the commodities unit) (Hall, 1999).

It is therefore always more profitable to maintain existing customers rather than try to acquire new ones. In fact, strengthening the relationship leads to a significant reduction of management and administration costs, thus contributing to the growth of profits over time.

6.8   Understanding the Role of the Customer

Given the difficulty of finding an univocal way of defining "CRM's universe," it is better to try and investigate its practical role, i.e. how it supports the different roles the customer takes up in his relationship with the provider: at any particular moment the customer must be considered in the most suitable way. CRM intervenes in an attempt to identify the correlation between these roles and the company business and provides the technological tools that will help the company to interface with the customers. A great many tools are available for the number of goals identifiable in customer support, so that the company will have to devise the right tool, for the right time, for the right "target" each time.

A simplified version of Griffin's table (Griffin, 1997) can be used to identify five main customer figures arranged in order of growing importance, from the standpoints of support required from the company, difficulty of task and, above all, profitability:

- Customer as a prospect,[27]
- Customer as a number,
- Customer as a business partner,
- Customer as an E-customer,
- Customer as an asset.

The first stage in the customer's life cycle is the prospect stage, when the company's aim is to turn him into an actual customer. In this phase a typical CRM tool comes up: SFA[28] software specifically allowing gathering and sharing of information about the customer even if it originates from several sources, functions or contacts, thus making it unnecessary to open too many files and spreading data and efforts, so as to manage the opportunity in the best possible way and to realize it with a purchase.

It is self-evident how an integrated CRM system, as opposed to the data islands often lost in company terminals, is a vital component in the management of an effective relationship with the potential customer.

The next stage, which is by no means the last, is to consider the customer in terms of a well-identified account, in which all the data concerning transactions carried out are recorded and maintained: in this way a powerful CRM tool, the *data warehouse*, comes to life. This is the basis for the development of a customer service with targeted marketing policies and for the implementation of other tools, such as *data mining* (Berry, Linoff, 1997; SCN Education B.V., 2001).

---

[27] Term used in marketing to mean a „potential customer".

[28] Sales Force Automation.

The attainment of the role of business partner (third stage) implies that CRM is definitely interpreted as a holistic vision of the customer's activity toward the company. An ERP[29] system that is able to monitor and support the company's performance at any given moment of the providing relationship makes it the basic core of CRM solutions. In order to treat customers as real partners it would be advisable to allow them access to the ERP system – through a self-service protected portal – both for reasons of transparency and to show an attitude of actually sharing and valuing the relationship. This system of real-time position checking can solve a number of problems that can come up, often involuntarily, concerning communication, procedural agility, etc.

Nowadays a new, internet-related way of doing business is emerging: many claim it will take over, but for the time being it is just one of many ways. E-Business requires tools and attitudes peculiar to itself, which simply did not exist even as little as 10 years ago. The CRM galaxy is just starting to adjust to this trend through a branch that will soon be self-contained, called E-Crm (West; 2001). Typical applications for approaching the customer are, among others, the *multichannel E-customer interaction management,*[30] *E-customer click stream analysis,*[31] *E-customer loyalty management,*[32] etc. E-CRM's main objective is the attainment of a fair level of integration among its components, in order to become an indispensable tool for web-active companies (Seybold, Marshak, 1999; Griffin, 1997; Brown, 2000).

It might be interesting to try and spot a possible life cycle for an entirely web-managed customer.

Every company employs resources to preserve the goods that make up its patrimony (this is the final step). The specific feature is that it was only with the introduction of CRM that many companies realized the importance of effective management of one of their most substantial goods: the customers (Blattberg, Getz, Thomas, 2001). In the CRM environment a number of companies are successfully implementing data mining and data warehousing systems, as already mentioned, knowing they will be better able to achieve their targets of customer satisfaction and trying to find new ways to increase the number and profitability of their cus-

---

[29] Enterprise Resource Planning: a software solution allowing direction of an organization's requirements in order to meet the company's needs through tight integration of all its functions.

[30] The multichannel 0E-customer interaction management is designed to manage relationships through all web-supported communication channels: chat, e-mail, voice service, fax, etc.

[31] E-customer click stream analysis analyses the customer's behaviour through the „stream of clicks" he leaves during his navigation sessions, in order to prepare ad hoc actions for the subsequent contacts.

[32] Customer loyalty management seeks to spot bonus and incentive policies for frequent web-buyers, in order to increase their visits to the site that rewards them.

Figure 6.7   Customer life cycle

tomers. Customers are in fact some of the cheapest and most reliable critics of acompany's activity, and analysing them with data mining tools can help to evaluate the direction the company is taking, as well as supporting the decision process.

Since all companies have an – often unused – transaction data recording system, it is easy to predict that they are all going to implement a CRM system in the future, given the innumerable advantages it offers. The first thing that has to be understood is what roles the customers can adapt in order to design a suitable architecture that reflects the company's actual needs. CRM is only successful if the customers see it as a single, consistent interface between themselves and the company, rather than as a number of disconnected and uninformed realities managing the relationship as autonomous units.

6.9   Satisfaction, Loyalty, and Defection

CRM recognizes that the customers are the core of a company's business, its success depending on how effectively the relationships with customers are managed. In order to do this, it is necessary for the company to know precisely who the customers are, and not simply know them as groups or macromarket segments – although this is sometimes a result in itself; persons within the company must know each and every one personally. The essence of CRM is the ability to give detailed answers including figures to such questions as: Is this a "good" customer? How profitable is he? Why is he doing business with the company? What does he especially like about us? Does he purchase from the competition as well? Competition on markets is very strong, and consequently one of today's leading imperatives is the necessity to manage relationships "at every contact point" in order to build up increasingly firm associations and thus be able to define the company's own customers as loyal and try to ensure that the loyal ones also become the most profitable (Griffin, 1997). To achieve this, the most sensible companies make strict choices among applications for their front-office[33] posts, since this is where the – often direct – contacts with customers take place (Keenan, 2001).

Satisfaction monitoring activities are certainly not something new introduced by CRM. It was empirically found that such an indicator is not sufficiently significant to allow predictions of the customers' future degree of loyalty. As a matter of fact, an investigation by META Group shows that 50% of the satisfied customers will do business with the competition in the near future, while as many as 25% of those who declare themselves very satisfied will soon switch to the competition (Burnett, 2001; Bielski, 2000).

Such percentages lead companies to investigate factors other than the satisfaction level, as this does not seem to be any conclusive guarantee of customers' future behaviour (Berry, 1983). To build up lasting relationships it is necessary to focus much more on the traces left by customers, in order to extract information and behave in keeping with this: it is said that the attitude must be proactive rather than reactive. To achieve a proactive approach it is necessary to count on an organizational structure which is strongly customer oriented and able to accomplish what CRM proposes (Egan, 1999; Brown, 2000).

The objective is, to quote an apt expression, "that the customers be induced to faithfully leave in outsourcing the greatest number of decisions possible to our company" (Keene, 2001; Brown, 2000); only in this way is the defection rate going to subside.

This problem, also known as the *"churn rate"*, is especially acute in a strongly liberalized and competitive market such as telecommunications. This phenomenon has a cost of approaching 4 billion Euros per year, which is sustained by the major European and American companies as new competitors enter the market, making offers targeted on certain segments or countries. Considering that it takes an average of 3 years to recover the loss generated by a lost customer through a new one, and that the defection rate can reach 25–30% each year, several firms active in this

---

[33] Examples are local branches, call centres, salesmen, etc.

industry will hardly generate satisfactory returns on their investments. The challenge faced by managers is to spot a priori the next likely *"churners"* and persuade them, through appropriate policies, to stick with their current company. Another aspect is the individuation at source of the most suitable methods of selecting new customers, focusing on those who are not likely to disappear as soon as someone else makes a better offer (Hall, 1999; Delmater, Hancok, 2001).

Policies and technologies used by CRM promise to provide a solid contribution to overcoming the perspective limits of customer satisfaction indicators, to lending concrete support for the achievement of customer loyalty, and to reducing defection rates (Gilmore, Pine, 2000).

7 Main Benefits and Organizational Impacts of CRM within the Bank

7.1 A New Business Organization

With the spread of the customer-oriented approach, the old concepts of "mass production" and "mass marketing" are giving way to new business models, in which customer relationships are acquiring a leading role (Gilmore, Pine, 2000):

- The life cycle of customer relationships is a key issue. *"Customer reten-tion"* and *"Customer profitability"* are becoming important elements in the achievement of wider business objectives such as the company's over-all profitability and the value increase for the investors (Rountree, 2001).

- New tools and technologies in the CRM environment, e.g. Inter-net/intranet, and data warehouses, offer new opportunities and a wider range of choices, allowing an enhanced information management and in-dividual customer relationships (Bielski, 2001).

With the development and spread of transmission networks, the Internet, telecom-munications, etc., companies are led to change their own organizational models in order to achieve full exploitation of the new opportunities provided by ICT's new technologies.

Table 7.1   A new business organization

	Stable environment	**More competitive environment**
Enterprise vision	Short term Product focused	Long term Customer focused
Organization	Hierarchical structure	New business processes and organization to take advantage of IT opportunities
Sales	Little customer knowledge Face-to-face selling	High customer knowledge, mass customization, multiple channel selling, E-commerce
After sales and service	Reactive Separate processes and organization	Proactive, integrated processes and organization

Speed and globalization are becoming necessary conditions of staying in the market, and are forcing companies to modify their own strategies and organization, to re-duce time-to-market and thus to operate real-time. A new model is introduced, the *extended company*, which models the constant contact of the company with its customers, providers, partners, and personnel. Precisely because of the availability of such new technologies, the old space and time barriers that used to regulate or limit competition collapse; there is therefore a need to re-design and rethink all internal processes, in order to (Brown, 2000; Burn, 1989; Galliers, Baets, 2000):

- Enhance competition capacity,
- Increase innovation capacity,
- Shorten reaction time for demanding changes,
- Improve profitability,
- Increase number, satisfaction and loyalty of own customers.

Companies are therefore searching for organization models:

- Oriented to the achievement of high standards of effectiveness, effi-ciency, flexibility and reactivity,
- Based on information sharing among customers, partners, and providers,
- In which customers' needs and expectations model the relationship sys-tem between the company and the outside.

7.2   CRM, IT, and Organizational Approaches

A fundamental role in the creation of the extended company falls to technology (Galliers, Baets, 2000; Ciborra, 2000; Fontana, 1995). As a matter of fact, the in-formation flow that used to link merely the main company functions (production, administration, marketing, etc.) now has to be extended to outside the company, taking advantage of the opportunities offered by fixed and mobile communication networks (De Marco, 1992).

The adaptation of this new business model will cause the switch from "structured company" to "virtual company", thus also modifying the market approach. There will be a transition from a "reactive" approach able to adapt quickly to changes in demand and competition to a "proactive" approach able to anticipate changes.

In this context, information on customers becomes a strategic resource. In the step from transaction to dialogue, the company must be sure to turn every contact with the customer into an opportunity to improve its own market knowledge, to define new ideas, to create loyalty, and to do cross- and up-selling, etc. (Smale, 2000).

This greater complexity has brought about an increased need for accurate and quick information, in order to create useful knowledge for use in future decision processes. Operational systems are also evolving in the direction of new models and applications, which often have Internet as an infrastructure and are centred on:

- The integration of front and back office systems,

- The management of information flow along the whole "value chain",

- Customer relationship management.

The focus is switching from the operational to the executive information systems. In fact, there is a growing spread of data warehouse systems, which contain the most significant data for the study of company activities, and of business intelligence systems, which allow managers to understand all cause-and-effect relationships at the base of the company's operation. This is called the knowledge management area, supporting knowledge generation and diffusion within the company itself.

7.3   Change Management and CRM Initiatives

The introduction of a CRM strategy can lead the company to:

- Change the traditional evaluation and approach modes concerning customers and markets. It might in fact open up entirely new markets or effect the abandonment of nonloyal or nonprofitable customers.

- Create new communication channels between the best customers and research or production areas. "This way the customers' suggestions and evaluations, originating from the actual use of products and services, can be used to maximize the company efforts to improve the innovation and creation capacity, according to the customers' preferences and needs" (PricewaterhouseCoopers, 2000). What is more, the company has to establish guidelines for managing channels in terms of:

- Service provision modes over all available channels – the company should be able to present a consistent image to its customers.

- Choice of the most suitable channels according to the customers' characteristics and preferences.

In contrast to the past, when companies could only refer to their sales personnel, they now have a whole range of other means available to contact its customers, which lead to new opportunities not just in terms of effectiveness, but in terms of efficiency as well, on a cost-per-contact basis (Nadin, Cerri, 1999). In fact, the cost-per-contact level will guide the choice of the customer interaction mode.

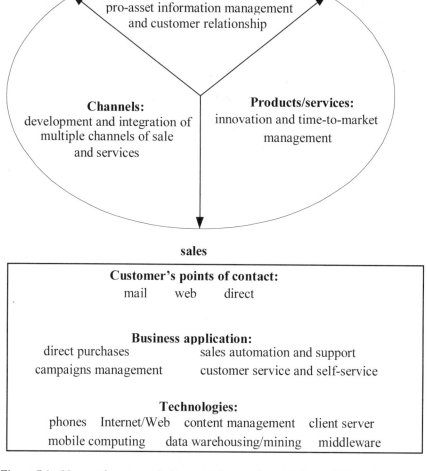

Figure 7.1   New market approach. Source: PricewaterhouseCoopers, 2000

The new customer contact approaches raise questions about the very nature of the current sales networks. Up to now, the salesperson has been considered the only actor entitled to cultivate relationships with customers. The latest management approaches, implying the use of call centres, for example, allow routine tasks in customer management (e.g. acquisition and carrying out of orders, payment control, etc.) to be given a lower priority than the search for new business opportunities. This makes it possible to maintain or even improve the quality of customer service while effecting significant cost reductions (e.g. fewer commissions for fewer salespersons) (Child, 1987; Brown, 2000).

Therefore, customer maintenance and management activities no longer fall in the exclusive competence of the commercial personnel, requiring on the contrary internal reorganization of company functions, from production to logistics, from sales to service, in order to meet the customer's demands in terms of schedule keeping, and product and service quality, etc. (Galliers, Baets, 2000).

To make the introduction of this new approach successful, companies must carefully consider the following key dimensions:

- Integration: concerns the development of a consistent and integrated channel strategy, supported by accurate analyses of the data relating to customers. The contribution of Business Intelligence is fundamental here, allowing for the combination of structured, mainly quantitative data with unstructured data, text or multi-media, owing to the recent opportunities provided by web technology. What is more, a new concept is coming about, that of the *"Enterprise Information Portal"* created using company intranet and extranet, supporting analysis, reporting, and decision activities for all the company's *knowledge workers* and partners.

- Balance: concerns the attainment of a balance in the use of the available collaboration technologies (self-service or operator-assisted interactions), bearing in mind the cost of each option and, above all, the customers' preferences.

- Technology: applies to the operational infrastructure, or the choice of the suitable technological components for the exchange, the gathering, the understanding, and the proactive use of customer information. It is a very important element in the introduction of new technologies which may turn out to be a great risk for the company. Therefore, it is recommended that prototypes be tested and that companies proceed step by step before implementing the new technologies on a large scale.

- Change management: the entire organization, from processes, to personnel, to infrastructures, etc., is involved in a radical change (Galliers, Baets, 2000; De Marco, 1992). It is necessary for the company to manage it cautiously, trying:

  - Not to underestimate the amount of required resources, from both a qualitative (competencies) and a quantitative (work loads) point of view,

  - Not to create unattainable expectations among the users,

  - To involve all interested areas in the project from the start, in order to come to agreements on objectives and functional requirements,

  - To promote customer orientation.

8 Data Mining Systems Supporting the Marketing Function: The Experience of Banca Monte dei Paschi di Siena

8.1 Introduction

The dynamics of economic activity, seen as gain, consolidation, and loss of market positions, has experienced a marked acceleration in the last few years, thus setting up a number of challenges for banks in relation to their future success (Rossignoli, 1995).

The main change factors, such as the growing international competition, triggered by new laws and deregulation processes, or the fast and steady technological, economic and demographic developments, have led to the following remarks:

- The intensity of knowledge present in products and services is in constant growth, causing high costs for all work linked to knowledge per product.

- The knowledge required by company processes experiences a rapid turnover, and its life cycle becomes shorter in several application areas.

- The time pressure under which decisions with a high grade of knowledge are taken is also increasing.

In order to face these changes, companies are forced to rethink their own knowledge management policies and to have recourse to the use of new tools to support certain strategic functions (such as marketing and management), answering a market demand that is constantly increasing in complexity and subject to rapid changes.

Given this scenario, all pieces of information that have the potential to cause company decision processes to achieve their business objectives are enjoying increasing importance.

This has brought about the opportunity to use, albeit to a different end, the huge information sources available to companies, particularly those operating in mass distribution, credit and finance.

In fact, in the last few years we have experienced an explosive growth in the systems' capability to generate and store data. The progress in information gathering through magnetic card readers, the spread of identification codes to cover just about every commercial product, the current use of credit and debit cards, and the huge volume of institutional transactions have brought about archives of a magnitude that was once unthinkable. This growth was helped decisively by the improvement of mass memorizing technology, with a consequent reduction in the cost of appliances, as well as by the refinement of DBMS and the creation of data warehousing strategies.

Such an amount of data, though, cannot be effectively or efficiently processed by traditional methods such as electronic sheets or ad hoc queries if the objective is to discover new knowledge and thus new connections between the available data, with the aim of enhancing the company's overall performance in all its operational areas. This explains the need to seek tools capable of performing an "intelligent" and automatic analysis of large databases and also capable of generating significant reports.

The techniques allowing attainment of these objectives are known as *Knowledge Discovery in Databases;* the present definition dates from 1989 and was formulated by Shapiro and Matheus during the first workshop dedicated to the subject. It covers the entire interpretation and research process of logical passages within databases, implying, as a crucial step, the coordinated application of specific data mining algorithms. These terms are used to indicate the number of techniques deriving from artificial intelligence, statistics, and scientific visualization used for the extraction of *knowledge*, i.e. information present in implicit form in the huge databases, in order to attain a better comprehension of the phenomena and behaviours that are the objects of the analysis, and to be able to predict future trends.

Set into this scenario is the study performed through the Marketmine project, which aimed to verify the applicability, as data mining techniques in the finance market, of *rule induction* and *neural networks*, which are specific theoretical and application fields of artificial intelligence and statistics (Wasserman, 1990).

8.2   Market Evolution

In the last few years the evolution of reference markets has been experiencing an acceleration that recently attained exponential peaks, after decades spent in a limbo impermeable to outside shocks where they lived a gratifying life of "competing" among a protected oligopoly.

The speed of this evolution can be explained by the fact that it has not come about as the result of any single propelling factor; actually each market component, often independently, has been affected by innovative phenomena.

These first began with legal and regulatory aspects, for, since the relevant laws were obsolete, the surveillance commission was forced to intervene in the 1970s and 1980s in order to regulate the new types of services and operations, given that the legislature lacked any desire to do so.

8.2.1   Operators

Market operators, besides undergoing an evolution, have increased in number as well as diversifying their provenance.

While banks were the absolute leaders up to a few decades ago, they have gradually been outflanked by intermediaries of nonbanking origin which, deriving their approach from the industrial sector they originate from, have brought about a new modus operandi characterized by such elements as strong sales motivation or a specific inclination to external communications.

8.2.2   The customer

There was a time when the customer used to consider investment safety the principal, if not the only, aspect that had to be considered in his choices. This virtually "forced" him to turn to banks, which, owing to their nature, seemed to be the only intermediaries able to guarantee it.

For a number of reasons, although mainly because of the virulent de-intermediation process triggered by the rise in inflation (which is still continuing today, albeit in concealed form), the Italian saver has also started to use remuneration as an evaluation meter for his choices.

The State's entry into the money market as a competitor, through the offer of Treasury Vouchers, has pushed on this "frantic" search for profitability further, also as the result of a strong inflation rate.

This competition was long fought over interest rates, in spite of the numerous interventions by the Surveillance Commission, which tried to introduce both authoritative correction measures (such as maximum ceilings for loans, compulsory reserve modifications, etc.) and structural ones (e.g. the introduction of deposit certificates aiming to stabilize the return rate).

The picture was then completed with the gradual liberalization of the market, by this time characterized by the principles of free competition and adapted to the new European frontiers, over which the customer finally "grew up" both in terms of independence and culturally, becoming conscious of his rights and his importance.

8.3   The Organization of Marketing Initiatives

The above would only be marginally important if we did not consider that the evolution of these and other, no less important, marketing components, have in fact determined a quick and parallel evolution of the so-called banking marketing.

In origin, in the absence of any significant ground motivations, banks, given their position as exclusive advisers to the customers, were merely used to adapting industrial marketing elements.

The subsequent diversification of offers triggered the development of specific product marketing applications, which were, however, initially oriented to the promotion of products/services marketed by one bank as opposed to the others, rather than to highlighting suitability of the products/services to satisfy actual customer needs.

A further push in this direction was given by the gradual market globalization, which, among all other consequences, affected a significant increase in the pressure from foreign competitors.

These are some of the circumstances that pushed the banks toward a customer-oriented approach. They are now focusing their attention more and more on the customers, trying to transform themselves into customer-centred organizations.

Such a model has lately undergone a further evolution, in order to allow the "refounding of the relationship" between bank and customer: new engineering seeking a new kind of loyalization based on customer satisfaction and, even more, on customer care based on matching customer needs (demand) and the products/services marketed (offer).

8.3.1   The Data

Any organization, be it a foundation, an association, or a company, operating with the public acquires a steady flow of data and information. Some of it is usually permanently stored in electronic archives (the ones necessary to the actual activity), while the rest is immediately used or stored on ephemeral supports (e.g. the data of a booking, an information request).

This state of affairs, however, is apt to change radically the moment there is a need for more profound knowledge of the customers, of their behaviour, and of their preferences.

The same data as formerly had a mere accounting or organizational value acquire primary importance and come to be a vital knowledge tool (especially if they are suitably aggregated to form information according to more or less complex structural models).

In the context of a consolidated and vaunted competitive attitude, the industrial and mass distribution sectors have long metabolized this concept, propelled by the need to develop their knowledge of acquired and potential customers. Banks, on the other hand, until lately, merely used the data flow in an operational way, namely to manage the relationships established with customers and their financial overflows or deficits.

This habit only subsided with the transition to a customer-oriented marketing model as banks became conscious of the need to use all the information they could get their hands on in a downright commercial way as well.

Unfortunately, along with the above, another, not-so-positive realization also emerged: the archives only contained the historical series needed in accounting or the ones that were compulsory by law, while all others kept getting lost.

8.4   The Bank

Such a bank has also undergone all marketing evolution phases, facing all change necessities rationally and immediately as they came up, as exemplified by our experience going back several centuries.

As long ago as in the early 1990s, the need to rationalize customer knowledge was felt, which was met by implementing a marketing information system (MIS).

After a long and useless search for an adequate support among the ones available in the market, it was decided to proceed with a proprietary realization, using internal resources and turning to outsourcing only for those modules that proved cheaper if provided by consultants and professionals available on the market.

In due course the two basic modules, the product catalogue and the customer file, were created and were subsequently joined by a search engine using an especially developed software, "Diogene", which now allows the use of the information system for a number of trade activities (e.g. monitoring of budget attainment, development and monitoring of commercial campaigns, customer segmentation).

This was not considered as an end-point, but much rather as a suitable starting ground. In a market characterized by increasing competitive dynamics, it is essential to ensure constant updating and enrichment of the MIS. This is just to enhance and maximize the information held, while at the same time looking for new analytical tools able to "read" all customers' needs and behaviours more effectively and, through these, all changes in the market's characteristics.

All the above elements are vital or the interpretation, and when possible anticipation, of the outcome of new needs on the market, with concrete achievements consisting in the marketing of new products/services, or simply in the restyling of old ones.

8.4.1   New Projects

This innovation objective was attained through the development of two separate projects, which had been in construction for some time: one was called "Customer Care Centre" and was totally internal, while the other, called Marketmine, was developed with the help of other partners of nonbanking origin, with the approbation of and input from the EC.

8.4.1.1   Customer Care Centre

This initiative was of strategic importance to the bank, as it aimed to create new, innovative trading channels (which were intended to join the existing ones in a multichannel distribution strategy) while also leading to the activation of a Marketing Intelligence function.

This function should use highly specialized resources as well as advanced methods and supports (such as data mining, neural networks, data warehouses), giving it a decisive importance in the enhancement of customer knowledge, meaning his characteristics as well as his unexpressed needs.

This in turn should originate an actual "quality leap", for it allowed the use, besides the traditional and well-known statistical analysis tools (simulations, market research, sample analysis, which used indexes, statistical averages, linear or multiple regressions), of data mining, which can be defined as *"a process of discovery and interpretation of rules and models present in the data in order to solve business-connected problems."*

Data mining allows the strategic marketing staff, among other things, to:

- Cluster customers,
- Evaluate purchase inclination,
- Evaluate the profitability of models and profiles,
- Evaluate and abandon causes,
- Optimize the use of banking channels.

8.4.1.2   Marketmine

The Bank's participation in the Marketmine project also belongs in the same context. This initiative involved a number of high-level partners, such as the Università Cattolica del Sacro Cuore, particularly its research centre named CeTIF – Financial and Information Technologies Centre, the PAC (Parallel Application Centre) of Southampton University, U.K., and Ais@ftware, a company based in Milan, Italy.

This project, the execution of which started at the end of 1997, was financed by the EC.

The goals it aimed to achieve are:

- The preparation of an integrated data mining environment, to be used in the banking industry to implement the technologies developed in the marketing area,

- The extension of the visual data mining tool, which was developed in the DB Inspector project,[34] so that it can hopefully support learning projects in the marketing area,

- The development of a substantive application in the financial industry allowing for the combined use of the different data mining tools in the available data processes,

- The production of a standardized demonstration protocol.

This is how responsibilities were shared out within the project:

- Ais@ftware was responsible for software development and coordination.

- PAC (Parallel Application Centre), a research centre of the University of Southampton, with expertise in rule induction, was to support Ais@ftware and CeTIF in prototyping and in project specifications.

- The Università Cattolica – CeTIF – was in charge of data analysis activities, which were performed in collaboration with the bank.

- Banca Monte dei Paschi di Siena SPA, finally, was the end user and responsible for preparing the data, defining all business requirements in detail, and evaluating the results.

The execution was carried out in three main steps:

---

[34] Another ESPRIT project funded by the European Community, Area 6, HPCN.

- **Preparation**

This included:

- – Definition of analysis models,
- – Identification and structuring of rules,
- – Verification of their validity,
- – Definition of the overall reference model.

- **Experiments**

Sample tests were be carried out on two branches featuring an equal development potential.

- **Analysis and evaluation**

The aim was to verify the actual profitability of these innovative techniques.

From a practical point of view, the results of this activity were quite significant, even going beyond the project's general and shared goals. This initiative allowed us to verify the actual profitability in the use of innovative project support techniques (neural networks, data mining, data warehouse, etc.) pragmatically by means of a real promotional activity, which was designed and created for this very objective.

The initiative was carried out simultaneously in two different environments (branches) that featured equal development potential, in the first case using the innovative techniques and in the second the traditional ones, to allow a comparison of the actual effectiveness, efficiency, and profitability of the aforementioned innovative and traditional techniques "in fieldwork".

This new experience, together with other initiatives, which were carried out within the bank and were no less important to the matter, allowed us to perform the three main investigation tasks in market intelligence, namely:

- **Reporting**

Or: what happened?

(Which products/services were placed, with which customers, in what zones, individually or in groups, in what particular periods)

- **Ad hoc queries**

Or: why did it happen?

(Why the budget was/was not attained, which customer groups have behaved in a certain way, etc.)

- **Predictive modelling**

Or: what is going to happen?

(How profitable is this relationship going to be? Which customers are going to leave us? Which products/services will be the most/least purchased? Which channels are going to be most profitable? What is the best product/channel/customer mix?)

All of the aforementioned is a further evolution of strategic marketing which, besides promoting higher efficiency of the overall commercial action, allowed, from a relational point of view, correct and effective combination of the three main actors in the trading activity: products/services, channels, and customers.

8.5   The Marketmine Project

The Marketmine project was part of the Esprit program, area 6 HPCN (High-Performance Computing and Networking).

This project was aimed at verification of the usefulness and applicability of data mining techniques for matters concerned with trading and marketing problems in the financial industry. In particular, the objective was the analysis of the data of Banca Monte dei Paschi di Siena, in order to produce customer segmentation for marketing purposes, and individuation of the customers who could potentially be interested in asset management products.

In the rest of the present chapter, we describe the approach used to construct a system able to seek out potential purchasers of managed savings products.

8.5.1   Analysis Methods

Although the fields of use are quite heterogeneous, some of the major data mining software producers and also several company–research institute joint ventures are presently trying, at a global level, to establish minimum standards concerning the arrangement of steps in the development of a knowledge discovery system.

The model contemplates the execution of a certain number of phases in a process that is by its nature interactive and iterative. It is interactive in the sense that one cannot expect to make significant discoveries simply through the automated elaboration of gigabytes of data (Mannila, 1997). Each phase of the process requires supervision by human experts, which is in fact of vital importance for the success of the experiment, especially at the stage of the choice of the data and variables to be submitted to the algorithms, and in the evaluation of the outcome. And it is

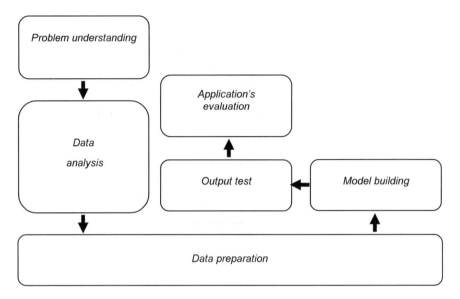

Figure 8.1   High-level schematic of the analysis model applied

iterative in the sense that some passages have to be repeated in sequence in order to approach the desired result through subsequent refinements (Bello, 2000).

In detail, it is possible to identify some of these phases in further passages, which gives the following process (Bello, 2000):

Step 1 – Clear definition and comprehension of the problem,

Step 2 – Acquisition, selection, cleaning and comprehension of the data,

Step 3 – Selection of a sample,

Step 4 – Construction of a customer profile,

Step 5 – Exploration and tuning of the variables,

Step 6 – Construction and application of the analysis model,

Step 7 – Testing of the outcome over the entire population,

Step 8 – Evaluation.

We can now proceed with the detailed description of each single step of the sequence, examining the actions that were subsequently undertaken in the development of Marketmine.

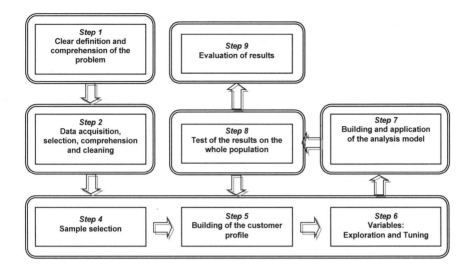

Figure 8.2   Details of the analysis model

8.5.2   Clear Definition and Comprehension of the Problem

The first step to be taken in a knowledge discovery process sequence is the definition of the problem. In fact, it is necessary to outline the environment's characteristics, the needs that led to the choice of the data mining tools and the objectives it
is wished to attain and the resources that will be made available in order to do it in
terms of data, personnel, application programs and implementation time. It is thus
possible to draw the logical trail to be followed during the development and consequently to determine unequivocally the business objective, avoiding excessive
generalization of the target, which would widen the application field unnecessarily
and reduce the significance of the results (Bello, 2000).

With the Marketmine project, BMPS's intention was to seek those elements that
would help to single out all customers with an inclination to purchase managed
savings products. This is part of a wider programme aiming to put the trading
function in a position both to have an active and a proactive attitude to the customer, and to understand where the action opportunities lie. This is to be
achieved also through the use of the most innovative techniques and with the help
of the information provided by Diogene, a tool from the bank's marketing area,
which was devised to simplify the set-up of the branches' trading policies,
providing them with the necessary support for objective and customer analysis.

8.5.3   Acquisition, Selection, Cleaning and Comprehension of the Data

One of the critical factors in success of data mining implementations is undoubtedly the datum and its consistency. To confirm this assumption, suffice it to consider that the preparation of inputs consumes the major part of the resources assigned to the development of the project in terms of budget, time, and personnel.

The acquisition of data requires first the individuation of the sources from which the information is to be extracted and subsequently the selection of the features potentially relevant to achievement of the planned objectives. Depending on the aim of the research, and thus on the particular family of algorithms chosen for the automated learning, certain specific items of information acquire more importance than others. For instance, it is well known that magnitudes measuring wealth are of greater discriminating importance for savings products, while, in order to segment customers where other products (e.g. credit cards) are concerned, behaviour variables prove more effective.

DIOGENE

The origin of the data required for the analysis activity is Diogene, BMPS's marketing database. It was created with the aim of overcoming the problems deriving from the reading and interpretation of the data present in the bank's archives. As a matter of fact, the marketing areas have a large amount of information available, which often proves difficult to read, for the data's structure is not designed to obtain a synthesis allowing better comprehension of the phenomena, and nor does it facilitate linking of the various aspects, which is left to the free interpretation of the single operator. Activities are therefore based on individual experience – which often leads to the examination of each single customer – and linked only by an abstract and simplified vision of the market position where one operates. The creation of Diogene aims to master problems of this kind, putting the marketing area in a position to "surf" among the information on offer, supporting the complex analysis and synthesis activities and thus allowing it to adapt an active attitude toward the market, setting up a consistent and coordinated trading policy that can take account of all the numerous variables that affect it.

In order to simplify the set-up of the branches' trading policies, the application provides the sales network with two particularly useful support tools allowing:

- Objective analysis,
- Customer analysis.

Through the first module it is possible to keep the degree of objective attainment of each branch steadily under control, thus enhancing the analysis of the discrepancies between objectives and actual results.

The second module allows the people responsible for the sales network's trading plans to monitor a number of especially significant events, in order to grasp the opportunities offered by the customers and single out the individuals whose behaviour is anomalous.

The cross-examination of these phenomena permits the identification of the intervention possibilities as well as of the causes of success or failure.

As a matter of fact, the objective analysis provides the trading area with steady and real-time information, so that it can react quickly to adjust its initiatives to the market's requirements, gaining a better chance of success.

Connection between the single pieces of information is made possible by the reading of the products/segments matrix, which allows a deep comprehension of the phenomena at a different level of detail. In fact, the matrix is designed to simplify the analysis of the customer segments, on which the branch's demand is focused, through a simplified scheme enabling it to find out, for each product, the nature and quantity of customers owning it, and the quantities and volumes in which they own it.

Diogene can perform this investigation according to five distinct classification criteria: customer marketing code, type of customer, Istat branch, socio-demographic segment and behaviour segment.

Through this tool, the trading areas can bear in mind, while examining the composition of the customer portfolio, several qualitative and evolutionary aspects that are not found in the accounting data.

This is especially useful both for making a targeted selection of the segments on which commercial efforts should be concentrated and for singling out those niches in which the bank has only a marginal presence or none at all, so that it does not have the information needed to evaluate the behaviour of the niche correctly itself.

Finally, the system provides a number of functions for monitoring the activities linked to the design and activation of commercial campaigns, as well as the results of these and the balance control of initiatives undertaken.

The availability of a data structure such as Diogene, created according to marketing needs and thus designed to support analyses in which the focus tends to move from product and transaction to the customer, has undoubtedly simplified the phase of knowledge acquisition.

In particular, the following tables have been considered: customers' file and commercial characteristics, details of operations carried out through the account service, bank's products' features, and products owned.

Customers' file and commercial characteristics

Each customer is identified by a unique code, which, in bank databases, is usually marked as the CIF (Customer Information File) code. There is then an aggregation code, which is used to separate private users from firms and institutions, as well as to allow the aggregation of all information concerning all the shared headings for the same individual. For our purposes, only individual actual persons have been considered. Beside personal data, the records contain information of a commercial nature (such as indications to do with income, goods owned, and any prohibitions or revocations).

Operations performed through the account service

These tables contain details of the transactions carried out by each customer through the account service. The movements are subdivided by object and entail the total inflows and outflows for each "owned" object, starting from the reference date, and also the averages for the previous year, the current year and the previous month.

Bank products' features

These tables are a synthesis of the characteristics of the products classified by the marketing area, with more detail of what stock, loans and credits are concerned.

Ownership of products

Each CIF code number includes not only the ownership data for every single product, but also all aggregations carried out for each single relationship established or service required. In banking jargon, a service is a function going back to a well-defined category of products or services (bank accounts, stock, portfolio management, etc.), while relationship means any single agreement signed with the bank, which may refer to one or more products. Therefore, for instance, a customer owning two ordinary accounts and a pension account has one service (the banking account), two products (the ordinary account and the pension one) and three relationships (two ordinary accounts and a pension account).

Thus, besides the information common to all elements, these archives contain some characteristics referring to some particular products (stock maturity dates, how much of a loan has been repaid yet, etc.).

After extracting from the marketing information system the tables constituting the input source for the knowledge discovery process, the next step was to convert their format to make it possible to transfer their contents from Diogene's elaboration environment to the data mining systems used in the project.

Much attention has been focused on the register data (CIF codes and aggregation codes used as identification for each single customer, date of birth, sex, code referring to occupation, branch used, etc.), on the account details (number and volume of inflow and outflow movements during the observation period and the previous month, along with all the averages) and, finally, on information concerning the ownership of products, services and relationships (product codes, service codes, quantities owned, whether payments are made punctually, dates of granting, any deadlines, limits on credit, etc.).

After acquiring the image of all or part of the bank's database, it is possible to proceed with preprocessing, in order to search for and eliminate eventual errors and inconsistencies from the starting data. This is an important step, for it also allows understanding of whether the information, which can potentially be used to create the overall customer profile, which will be in turn used for rule induction by the data mining algorithms, is "robust" and thus reliable (Bello, 2000).

In fact, a complex analysis work requires consolidated and "clean" data, if possible devoid of errors attributable to inaccurate survey or recording, default values, special values given to an attribute to identify particular situations, or attributes only rarely evaluated. The data quality is thus essential to the attainment of correct conclusions that can be generalized from a limited sample to a whole world of individuals.

To support these activities, it was necessary to proceed with counting the recurrences of values for all the attributes considered. Some calculations and statistics of the same attributes were needed, both in order to appreciate the quality of the data from the various sources and to promote an overall vision of the leading characteristics of the population under analysis. In fact, a count of all categories of customers and products was carried out through simple SQL queries. Some averages and variances were also computations with the aim of discovering all the characteristics peculiar to the population sampled and verifying whether there were any particular market niches.

Thus, from the statistical projections and graphic representations based on the data from the MIS (marketing information system) it was found that, except for the preponderance of the "other private subjects" category, which was due to a mistake by the operators (the correct information was not inserted, for this category is a default value), the most densely populated classes are those of lower level employees, retired persons, and professionals.

What is more, a direct relationship was pointed out between the ownership rate of managed savings and the saving ability, especially for Ducat products and wealth management, although on average these products have a low access threshold.

8.5.4   Selection of the Sample for the Use of Data Mining Systems

Definition of a sample is required to allow the data mining algorithms both to learn the rules within an acceptable time and to simplify their training by providing a set of balanced examples, including a suitable number of cases for every whole that is to be classified, so that the conclusions may be as close as possible to the actual situation (Bello, 2000).

The direct application of knowledge discovery techniques to all entities present in the company archives (in this case the customers) would in fact be exceedingly costly and inefficient, for, given the huge number of recorded occurrences, it would lead to unacceptable response times.

Therefore, it is necessary to seek some selection criteria that are able to reduce the number of sampling elements without spoiling the actual proportions between the parts of the market niches that are the object of the analysis.

The said selection can be carried out across geodemographic (location of the customer in a certain area), social (limiting the analysis to certain age and income classes, or to certain professions), or behaviour characteristics (number of transactions carried out in a given period).

The population sampled for the analysis refers to the branches in an area of central Italy, and it was chosen because it was believed to be representative of typical BMPS customers. About 79 000 customers were involved in the census.

Only CIF codes referring to individual persons, along with their co-headings, have been contemplated, with companies left out of the analysis, for the objective is to get to know the individual customers' market potentialities.

At this point, an important choice had to be made: whether to aggregate the data concerning co-headings and single individuals, to obtain a complete file for each individual, or to consider them separately to avoid redundancies. The last option was chosen, in agreement with the bank's experts.

8.5.5   Construction of the Customer Profile

The conclusion of the preprocessing phase triggered the construction of a file in which each record includes all the information concerning a single CIF code, be it an actual person or a co-heading. The preparation of this is necessary as it constitutes the basis for the selection of a set of observations called the training set, upon which the data mining algorithms are to carry out their knowledge discovery task, trying to spot all possible logical schemes concealed in the data starting from a limited number of real examples.

In this way, all relevant data concerning each single customer are collected in a single database, so that they are easy to access, queries and extractions are quicker, and the overall vision promotes a better comprehension of the data and the immediate spotting of certain anomalies.

What is more, the use of such a structure places the emphasis on the central role of the customer; the data are reorganized starting from operational systems, which were designed simply to record all customers' activities. The effort made with Diogene, and starting from it, is about reusing these information sources in order to understand in depth WHO the customer is and WHAT can be done to satisfy him and thus enhance the profitability of the marketing campaigns promoted by the bank.

Once the archive with the customers' profiles was set up, all CIF codes that had proved active in the previous year, i.e. all customers owning at least one product who had carried out transactions through the account service, were selected.

For the construction of the customer file, some fields have been extracted directly from the tables provided by BMPS, while others have been obtained through elaboration of the fields contained in the tables themselves. Subsequently, all available register information was added, along with totals and averages referring to the use of the accounts.

The next step was to try to quantify the customers' finance potential, in order to subdivide them into segments on the basis of their saving capabilities. This measure is notoriously important in this kind of analysis, where the variables referring to wealth have the greatest discriminating effect. The average saving was calculated as an algebraic sum of the average monthly inflow and outflow movements originated in the stock and account services.

Other fields have been created instead to provide an indication of the yearly inflow and outflow movements and their differences, so as to help outline each customer's actual economic capabilities.

Other information has also been included, concerning the duration of the customer's association with the bank from the moment the relationship was established, the number of days' ownership of managed savings, and the number of bank products owned, the last subdivided into traditional and managed savings products.

For some product classes, it was deemed necessary to create ad hoc ownership indicators (credit cards, ATM, stock), as for the major managed savings families, such as some types of life insurance, wealth management, Ducato common investment funds and two varieties of accounts featuring the automatic investment of deposit surpluses when these pass a predefined threshold.

Finally, the bank required the introduction of a further series of variables concerning product subdivision in terms of *Risk, Propensity to delegate investments,* and *Access threshold,* as this was thought to be important for the goal of customer segmentation.

Risk is a magnitude of the financial risk linked to the customer's ownership of each product. From this point of view ownership of a share is undoubtedly riskier than ownership of a savings deposit, for while in the first case the investment leads to an uncertain gain, and might even make a loss, in the second case the capital will remain untouched and its gains are quantifiable a priori.

Propensity *to delegate investments* refers to the grade of independence applied by the customer in the management of his investment. The more he delegates the management of his goods to the bank, the higher the delegation grade. In our analysis we have used the opposite indicator, namely the level of *Autonomy*: the more the customer delegates to the bank his goods' management, the lower his autonomy level.

The *Access threshold* indicates the minimum investment required to access a certain product. For instance, a credit card has an access threshold lower than that needed for obligation stock, for its provision cost is lower.

Each index has been associated with an overall value (high, medium, low). Each product is characterized by three values, according to the three indices mentioned above. The majority of customers who own managed savings products have a medium propensity to delegate investments and a low access threshold.

From the range of products owned it has been possible to reconstruct for each customer the indices for the overall and average values of risk inclination, delegation and saving capability.

It has to be stressed that the profile's structure is subject to the addition or subtraction of certain variables, according to the indications coming from the partial results in the subsequent iterations of the data mining process.

The obtained sample is composed of about 13 500 CIF codes, 2200 of which refer to customers who are owners of managed savings products.

8.5.6   Exploration and Tuning of Variables

This step, too, requires the use of statistical and scientific visualization tools to extract and represent the characteristics of the population sample that has become part of the training set.

In this way it is possible to obtain an immediate outline of the status of all variables, which is a great help in comprehending the starting situation. A further benefit deriving from the examination of the selected indicators lies in the fact that some links and relationships among them may emerge from the graphic representations and statistical briefs, which, through the addition of new magnitudes and the subtraction of existing redundant ones, allow highlighting of those factors that are most likely to influence the classification work.

It is also possible that examination of the sample will show the need to set new value intervals for the variables, in order to obtain a more homogeneous distribution of them, thus enabling the data mining algorithms to infer and provide more accurate answers.

8.5.7   Construction and Application of the Analysis Model

The two main tasks for data mining are to forecast future movements and to describe the current data. The forecasting activity implies the use of some variables or database fields in order to determine unknown values and future trends (Fayyad, Shapiro, 1996). The description activity, which is the most popular goal in knowledge discovery, requires the search for models allowing the final user to interpret the data easily and quickly or to uncover concealed logical schemes, which are the potential source of new knowledge.

Forecasting and description are carried out through the application of techniques such as classification, regression, and clustering.

The analysis model allows for the use of two data mining systems: the *Kohonen networks,* a particular variety within the family of neural networks, and *rule induction*. These algorithms have been chosen to answer two fundamental requirements:

- The need to segment customers anyway, leaving out considerations over ownership of managed savings products and any other a priori conjectures,

- The need to explain the criteria for the classification of customers into different classes.

The Kohonen networks prove particularly effective for the first requirement, as they are able to assign a different class to each element of a starting set (the customers in our case) on the basis of the combination of values in each element's attributes.

These techniques are, however, limited in that they are not capable of explaining the factors common to the elements belonging to the same class. For this reason it was decided to use the rule induction algorithms, which, on the contrary, allow extrapolation and easy interpretation of the rules that have led to the classification and that clarify the distinction between the owners of managed savings products and other customers.

8.5.7.1   Kohonen Networks

Among the most popular techniques used in data mining applications for the financial industry we find the *neural networks*, which are more or less complex systems, made up of very simple, properly interconnected elements called neurons. They have been designed to simulate, if in a very limited way, the flexibility, adaptation, and generalization characteristics of the human brain, which prove indispensable to the solution of a number of actual problems. At the basis of their development, there is the *connectionist* theory, according to which knowledge and behavioural processes are products of the interaction of very simple elemental modules.

We may therefore schematize an artificial neural network as a set of units, the neurons, linked to each other according to several possible patterns. From the final user's point of view, the network is just a black box to which a certain input is entrusted so as to obtain a certain output, without caring about the way this objective is achieved.

The success of these methods in the banking industry is due to their ability to perform nonlinear forecasts and extrapolate logical passages from data even in the presence of mistakes or incomplete examples, which is not infrequent in many banking application domains.

As already said, a neural network is made up of a large number of interconnected units, each of which is the equivalent of a biological neuron. Every unit receives several inputs from the others, upon which it elaborates a function called *transfer function*, thus producing an output that will be made available to the nodes it is linked to.

A neural network is not programmed but trained, which implies that it must be provided with input–output pairs without explaining how this is to be obtained.

There are two learning modes. The first one, based on progressive correction of the mistakes the network makes, is called *supervised learning*, since this phase requires the presence of a supervisor to correct the network as it provides wrong answers. The second method, *unsupervised learning,* is not based on the use of correct answers; in this case, the system analyses all inputs searching on its own for the common characteristics in order to form a set of classes.

In short, the unsupervised learning process has no use for input–output example pairs or, therefore, for a supervisor, since the training process is based on analysis of the inputs alone. The network must try to single out the analogies that might unite the inflow data, in order to obtain a certain number of sufficiently distinct classes that can adequately represent the application domain.

The Kohonen (1990) networks have been chosen as unsupervised learning tools for construction of the analysis model upon two prerogatives:

- They are able to learn, generalize, and provide the correct answer on the basis of a not only limited, but also incomplete or "noisy" example set.

- These maps can be dedicated exclusively to the learning, by finding relationships between inputs with no need to provide a priori learning outputs.

8.5.7.2   Rule Induction

One of the problems in the use of neural nets is the great difficulty in understanding the motivations that have led to a given classification, a task that can typically be thought as the search for a correct assignment of certain objects to categories determined by their characteristics.

Let us consider, for instance, a system for the authorization of credit card transactions: the characteristics examined will be the details of the proposed transactions along with the customer's behaviour profile, while the classes will be represented by the granting or nongranting of the credit.

In a classification model the connection between classes and characteristics can be defined simply, using flow diagrams, or in a complex and unstructured way, with manuals. Models can be obtained in two ways in principle: either by acquiring the necessary knowledge from experts in that field, or through *induction,* i.e. by generalizing specific examples.

In a typical induction example, we find, at ground level, a universe of objects, each characterized by a set of *attributes*. Each attribute gives the measure of one of the object's characteristics and takes up discrete and mutually exclusive values. Each object of the universe considered belongs itself to a closed system of mutually exclusive *classes*. We know a priori the belonging class of a certain object subsystem of the universe, which is called the *training set* (Quinlan, 1986).

Induction's crucial task is to try to extrapolate *classification rules*, in order to assign each object in the considered universe to its class according to the values of its attributes.

Rule induction is a complementary technique derived from artificial intelligence and statistics, allowing identifying relationships between data and expressing them by means of rules or decision trees. The latter are successfully used in supervised learning systems to classify objects into a closed number of classes. The tree's knots are labelled with the attributes' names; the branches represent the different values the attributes can have, while the leaves stand for the classes. In order to classify a case, we follow a route that starts from the tree's root, passes the knots and reaches one of the leaves. One drawback of decision trees is that they tend to attain remarkable dimensions, which makes their interpretation in actual applications awkward, for in the real world the number of attributes, each with a wide range of possible values, often becomes remarkably high.

In order to face this problem several alternatives have been studied, such as the subdivision of the original tree into a hierarchy of subtrees or the conversion of the classification model into *production rules*, the latter strategy enjoying an ample consensus.

Generally, the production rules take up the shape *IF L THEN R,* where *L* is a propositional expression, e.g. an expression in normal conjunctive form, that is to say a conjunction of tests on the attributes, while *R* indicates the assignment to a specific class.

In order to classify an example by means of this model, we must examine the ordered rule list until we find the one that contemplates our case in its conditional part. If none of the rules contemplates it, we will have to assign it to the default class previously established as the class recurring more frequently in the training set.

Apart from being easy to interpret, production rules have the advantage of being modular, which means that each rule is easily comprehensible on its own with no need to refer to the other ones.

Another significant advantage of rule induction over other approaches is the easy interpretation of the rules produced, which allow the achievement of a clear interpretation of the classification obtained even if the users have a limited knowledge of the application domain and a poor acquaintance with the basic theory upon which the algorithms are based.

The algorithm used is a rule induction program for the discovery of relationships and the classification of elements within databases of great magnitude. It produces either *decision trees*, graphic structures representing the possible classifications of the elements of a set, or *decision rules*, such as:

IF condition THEN belonging class.

Through an iterative process, the algorithms gradually classify all the examples present in the training set until the classification is carried out by analysing the values that the variables' attributes can possibly have.

Owing to the easy interpretation of the rules produced, which can be considered separately, to the relative response speed of these algorithms, and to the remarkable help provided by these rules in interpretation of the concealed logical schemes, the decision was taken to use rule induction as well as a data mining tool.

8.5.7.3   Scientific Visualization

The latest visualization techniques are used to convert a large amount of information to graphic representations, which are easy to understand and interpret because that visualization stimulates perceptive rather than cognitive reasoning.

Three possible approaches provide indications for the possible uses of these tools (Keim, Krisgel, 1993).

The first is about applying visualization to data mining, i.e. using these techniques to present the results obtained by means of specific data mining algorithms. The use of modern three-dimensional representation techniques makes it easier to spot clusters and data correlations.

The second approach consists in applying data mining to visualization; the implicit assumption here is that it is easier to apply search algorithms to a number of subsystems represented by graphic entities than to a vast and complex database. A significant example of this is the case in which multidimensional representation is used to select the attributes relevant to the search's objectives.

The third approach suggests the use of visualization as a support to data mining in the search for logical schemes and correlations between data.

For effective application, apart from profound knowledge of the domains on which the analysis is to be performed, the data mining algorithm requires technical knowledge of the specific methods that are to be applied. What is more, although these techniques are usually applied in a semi-automated way, the whole process, involving first the selection of the data and then the preparation and interpretation of the results, often turns out to be slow and onerous.

The three-dimensional visualization tools provide an alternative way of quickly analysing large amounts of information and thus quickly learning about characteristic data distributions. It is only necessary to think of the effectiveness of geographic views, which allow highlighting the distribution of certain facts over the territory.

In the development of the project, these techniques have been used to support preprocessing and for construction of the profile, in order to represent all selected variables and effect immediate highlighting of their distribution.

8.5.8 The Analysis Model

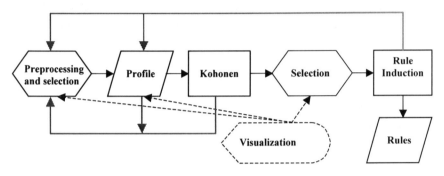

Figure 8.3   The analysis model. Source: Bello, 2000

In the method chosen for the data mining application, the training set, consisting of a selection of the sampled customers' profiles (all those who carried out at least one account movement during the reference period, and thus own at least one product), is submitted to analysis by Kohonen networks, which effect an unsupervised classification of the provided input in the absence of any indication of the desired output. The outcome is a field that has to be added to the profile and contains the coordinates of the class assigned to each element (each class is ideally represented by a field in a two-dimensional matrix).

In order to discover the motivations that have induced the network to assign a given customer to a given class we subsequently use the rule induction algorithm. The latter, based on the analyst's indication of the desired classification output (ownership or nonownership of managed savings), produces a list of rules describing the characteristics of the whole's various subsets, assigning them to one class or another.

The quality of the obtained rules is measured both in terms of the absolute number of classified examples and as a relationship between the number of examples correctly classified by the rule compared with the total number of examples it has been able to "capture".

The final objective is to obtain a set of rules applying to the entire population, making it possible to spot the customers with the strongest inclination to purchase managed savings products by way of a process that is both interactive and iterative. (It is interactive because it implies the evaluation of the results and the choice of the inputs for each step of the procedure, and iterative because at the end of each cycle several parameters have to be adjusted and some of the steps, repeated, for a gradual approach to the desired result.)

8.6   Marketmine: Project Results

The outcome of the research has been judged positively by the bank's experts, who have picked up some cues for the preparation of a pilot commercial initiative.

Particular interest was aroused by the result of the superimposing of the ownership data concerning the three main managed savings categories (life insurance, management of financial assets) and the classification produced by one of the Kohonen network iterations.

As for life insurance in particular, the algorithms have concentrated the owners in some segments, while others are almost completely lacking any managed savings products.

The rule induction algorithms were therefore applied to these particular classes, in order to find the rules describing their composition. A measure of the quality of each new-found rule is the relationship between the number of positive examples (in our case, owners of managed savings products) and the total number of examples captured, whether positive or negative, in other words all customers, no matter to which objective class they belong, who have the characteristics expressed in the conditional part of the rule.

In order to evaluate their accuracy, statistical functions have been applied in attempts to understand whether the rules generated were not influenced by the training set. This allowed an in-depth evaluation of the goodness of the generated patterns.

More generally, the objective is the maximization of the left diagonal of the "confusion matrix". With this matrix, the rows are used to show the data on the classification obtained with the analysis model, while the columns show the data on the correct classification of the sample, which is known a priori. The cases that are correctly classified by the model can thus be found in correspondence with the matrix's main diagonal.

The following tables show the results of the first experiment as described above.

Table 8.1   Results of experimental application of rule induction to a whole subsample

Model/target	# RG	RG	Model total	Model %
# RG	9 773	1 226	10 999	**82.1%**
RG	1 477	920	2 397	**17.9%**
Target total	11 295	2 146	13 396	
Target percentage	**84.0%**	**16.0%**		100.0%

Table 8.2   Results of experimental application of rule induction to a whole subsample, specifying proportions of false classifications yielded by use of the matrix.

Model/target	# RG	RG	
# RG	*88.9%*	*11.1%*	*86.9% wrong RG*
RG	*61.6%*	*38.4%*	*42.9% right RG*

It emerges from Table 8.1 that, when rule induction was applied to the whole sample a subset containing 2397 CIF codes was selected from the starting number of 13 396 (17.9%), 920 of which referred to customers who own managed savings products (out of 2146, ca. 42.9%). Among the 10 999 elements discarded by the rules, being considered not inclined to purchase managed savings products (82.1% of the training set) 126 turned out on the contrary to own such products.

While, on the one hand, the model estimated a distribution of managed savings products very close to the actual one ("Model percentage" column and "Target percentage" row), on the other hand it identified only 42.9% of the total managed savings and 88.9% of owners of such products correctly.

The rules allowing such results excluded from the training set all multiple headings, all customers with a generally low income, those owning payment cards and even having an account and stock budget, and those not owning payment cards and with a medium to low account and stock budget.

Based on these first results, a second experiment was carried out on the basis of the same data set updated to a second reference point. On the occasion of this updating, the calculations of the database statistics were repeated to follow the dynamic evolution of the study population, and the previously obtained results were verified, confirming the performance of the previously found rules applied to the fresh data.

The previous rules were thus applied to the new set, in order to verify their validity.

The total percentage of customers who had managed savings reached 39.49% (1268/3211).

In order to improve the accuracy of the results, it was then decided to update the customer profiles according to the following modes:

- Classification of the products in categories with the same value of *Risk, Autonomy, Access Threshold*, and introduction of indicators of ownership for these,

- Addition, as suggested by the bank's experts, of new indicators measuring, for each CIF code, the volume and number of movements of the stock service and the percentage relationship between the stock service and the overall account service,

- Transition from a set of prudent values to the subdivision into classes of the attributes concerning *length of time so far as a customer, stock volume, total stock movements, percentage relationship stock/(stock + accounts)*, in order to simplify the induction process, which can benefit from the treatment of variables that take up only a narrow set of values. The classification involved attempts to make the numbers in the obtained sets uniform.

The analysis was subsequently carried on using the previous model until the Kohonen network was applied, and was then continued according to two different approaches at the same time.

- By combining the subsets found by the Kohonen networks, two new sets were created, with respectively the highest and lowest concentration of managed savings,

- Other training sets were created for separate study of the classes with the highest percentage ownership of Ducato, wealth management, and life insurance products.

This course of action was designed to yield better overall description of the managed savings owners' segment, and of all other customers who do not appear to be inclined toward this type of investment; a further objective was a clearer definition of the ownership niches for each single product.

It was thus decided to apply the rule induction algorithms to these new subsets separately and in parallel.

It was possible to obtain new, more effective classifying rules, which individuate several categories of customers with no inclination to purchase our target products, having used the two subsets with the highest and lowest managed savings rate as training sets for the rule induction search. In fact, these rules make it possible to attain a set of customers in which the number of managed savings owners is higher than the one shown by the previous rules.

Let us now examine the results obtained with the help of the following Model/target consistency tables.

Table 8.3   Model/target consistence table

Model/target	# RG	RG	Model total	Model %
# RG	5 926	463	6 389	**46.8%**
RG	4 584	2 665	7 249	**53.2%**
Target total	10 510	3 128	13 638	
Target percentage	**77.1%**	**22.9%**		100.0%

Table 8.4   Model/target consistence table

Model/target	# RG	RG	
# RG	*92.8%*	7.2%	**56.4% wrong RG**
RG	63.2%	*36.8%*	**85.2% right RG**

The new set of rules selects a group of 7249 customers, representing 53.2% of the training set. Of the "captured" customers, 36.8% turn out to be managed savings owners, while the remaining 62.8% do not own any such products.

Compared with the results obtained by the previous iterations, the new rules have captured a greater number of customers, operating a "coarser" selection procedure on the sample, yet doubling the percentage of correctly spotted managed savings owners (85.2%).

The new rules excluded all the customers who appear to use their account just as a reserve for the payment of current expenses, those with a low "income" not using payment cards and not establishing long-term loans, and finally, those with a medium income, no payment cards, and just one support account.

Compared with the previous outcome, a slight worsening of the ratio of owners of *managed savings owners* to owners of *any product* (from 39.49% to 36.9%) was compensated by a doubling in the percentage of secured managed savings owners, from 41% to 80.7%.

At the end of the analysis, this final set was labelled as the group of customers who will potentially purchase managed savings products.

If we apply the rule that excludes all customers effecting a medium high yearly overall account movement to this set, we get a set containing 4338 elements, 2033 of whom, i.e. 46.86%, own managed savings products.

In this way it is possible to retain 64.78% of the managed savings in profile.

These results have allowed BMPS to conduct two parallel marketing campaigns, in order to verify the validity of the rules obtained; the first campaign uses the CIF codes shown by the data mining algorithms, while the second is carried out using traditional methods.

9 Conclusion

9.1 The Meaning of CRM

As already mentioned, the concept behind this acronym has a wide meaning and is particularly difficult to define. The different definitions proposed in the introductory section helped us to delineate at least the conceptual framework of the CRM.

The first important milestone has been to establish the nature of CRM. Most well-known researchers are currently agreed that CRM is a customer-oriented business strategy that involves many business units. As shown in the case studies analysed, such projects involve the IT and sales departments, marketing personnel and public relations staff as well as top and middle management. This emphasizes the complexity of implementing such systems and makes it clear that it is not possible to consider them as simple technological projects or as an application that will be useful in "pushing" sales.

Without going into the details again, it seems useful to propose some more thoughts on the components behind the acronym CRM:

Customer: it is the first term to that should be considered because, as stated above, reaching the customer is the aim of every company. After the adaptation of such a CRM system, this becomes even more important. The customer undergoes a transformation: starting from a generic role of purchaser, he first becomes a business partner and then turns out to be the most important subject in evaluating, correcting and improving the company's outputs. At any rate, the companies try to value the asset of the buyer in every way. When these policies are followed there is even a consistent benefit for the consumer himself.

Relationship: this component complements the previous one. The most important challenge of CRM is in fact adding value to the relationship with customers. In this context, relationship means a long-lasting relationship that undergoes a thoroughgoing transformation over time. Such relationships derive from a planned or even an unplanned occasion ("first contact"); they develop thanks to a reciprocal discovery ("collecting information"); they become progressively stronger (first purchase or transaction); they go through critical periods (complaints, tempting offers from competitors); and after an unforeseeable period they come to an end (customers change their suppliers, the company stops production). It is not very natural for a company to recognize this occurrence, just because companies are not human beings! People "inside" the organization should attempt to arrange conditions so as to make it possible to recognize the end of a customer relationship.

Management: even this word is coloured by what has been mentioned above. Relations with customers can arise spontaneously, but they can just as easily be broken off if the supplier does not monitor and "nurture" them in the right way. Customers do not go on buying from companies that do not meet their needs. In such a large competitive market as the present one, they can easily find other companies that offer a wide range of interesting products and services.

Two main topics relating to the management of relationships with customers are considered in this book: the technologies and the organizational impacts of the adapted strategies.

9.2   The Adaptation of Data Warehousing in a CRM Project

Any company considering the implementation of a CRM project must possess an adequate technological infrastructure. The first step is an effective data usage and storage system. The adaptation and implementation of a data warehouse is a common feature of all the case studies presented in the book. Apart from the definition adapted, in discussing inputting, processing, managing, publishing and validating business data, we definitely referred to database processes. The main problem to emerge was that of the so-called data in jail, meaning the impossibility of turning data into useful and reusable information. Such a state of affairs may appear incredible, but is actually a common situation encountered in many companies. Mostly data, information and skills are still present in the organization system, but because of structural and technological deficits companies often lose work, and with it also chances of profit.

Once more we feel we must point out that data warehouses do not in fact only carry out mere executive operations, but also support strategic planning and cost-controlling activities. Establishment of a data warehouse is undeniably a step on the way to a real CRM project. Moreover, data mining and OLAP applications also cannot perform their functions properly if they are not integrated with a good data management and storage system.

As already described, the process of building up the data warehouse architecture consists of different steps. Software and computers alone do not create a data warehouse project. In addition, metadata increase the structure's reliability and establish the inner rules of the system. On the one hand, the quality of the information must be monitored. These are both two examples of the problems and issues that must be considered when developing a process of data warehouse architecture. On the other hand, they confirm that the quality of the project does not rely exclusively on the types of software or the processing power of computers. This is why top management was the main sponsor in the experiences described. The IT staff, on the other hand, were the only persons concerned who were aware of the infrastructure needed, and were even the ones who updated and adjusted the internal processes before starting on a CRM project together with the organization department.

9.3   Using Data Mining in CRM Projects

Data mining has a fundamental role in the development of CRM project. As its aim is the analysis of business data, it necessarily goes along with data warehouse implementation. Good data analysis can in fact be performed only if a consistent, homogeneous, and complete database is available.

Starting from this premise, data mining architecture can be implemented. This cannot simply be seen as one phase in the CRM project. It is a related micro-project within the macro-CRM process. Data mining tools deliver an important additional value, which is the transformation of data into information and knowledge. Concrete applications of the information produced are, for example, sales campaigns based on different customer profiles and marketing plans focused on specific groups of customers. Such systems can outline targeted and small consumer groups, but individual consumer profiles can also be described in detail.

9.4   Theoretical Foundations of CRM

In this section, our intention is to try to understand whether actions and choices of companies engaged in these projects correspond to the theoretical organizational model that has been considered the best performing one in a CRM context.

Further comments on the examples discussed are presented in the following pages. Even though they do not emphasize the positive features of the models presented in the case studies, some interesting issues emerge.

Both theory and case studies have demonstrated that top management plays a crucial, wide and well-defined role in CRM projects. This group must be in total agreement on the idea of introducing such a thoroughgoing change in the company and must consistently support the project by constantly monitoring, checking, sponsoring and leading the transformation process. A particularly delicate situation arises when there are controversies between individuals or internal functions. Such conflicts can undermine the success of the project to a dangerous degree. Therefore, in these situations, top management must arbitrate, and must be able to solve all problems quickly. From a theoretical point of view, this implies strategic decisions that allow "dominating" both the organization and the external environment.

The operational part has an active role even if it is not directly involved in the CRM project, and it must not be left out. On the contrary, the positive effects of CRM must be accepted, and even supported, by the operational information system.

Following treatment of the areas directly involved in projects such as the improvement of relationships with customers, some considerations about the core of value and its functions are due. The core of an enterprise is the factor that induces customers to buy what the company produces. In such a context the middle manager and, above all, the front-office personnel must give proper emphasis to the business core, driving up sales and brand loyalty and dissuading customers from trying rival products and so on. Considering the difficult activity they are in charge of, managers should be aware of the great responsibility they bear, and in a wide sense they should be adequately stimulated and valued.

According to Thompson's theories, CRM may be considered as a number of activities aiming to overturn the temporal sequence in the interaction between organizations and their environment. It allows the mitigation of environmental impacts by creating a more stable and efficient technical core.

Companies that intend to implement a CRM system must have a clear attitude to external factors. Enterprises that believe in success obtained thanks to consistent attention to transformations and to events occurring outside the company boundaries have to invest in several different distribution channels. The theoretical model of satellites that turn around the organization confirms the same approach and fits in with the assumptions made in the case studies described. The use of this 'astronomy' simile suggests that these satellites, whilst smaller than and dependent on the main planet, benefit the planet itself in important ways, such as balance and the opportunity of keeping alive.

With reference to the significance of the aforementioned organization satellites a further remark is due. They represent all the resources that can be concentrated in the organizational area, where they are most needed. In other words, the satellites can be defined as buffers that make the organization ductile, flexible and dynamic. The whole of the organization and the market benefit from them. In fact, buffers form a sort of area within the organization where any strains arising are immediately dampened down. Moreover, their reshaping ability fulfils the fifth organizational construction described by Mintzberg.

As far as technologies are concerned, the main aspect that has to be considered is that they are an essential factor in CRM architecture, even if they cannot guarantee fulfilment of the planned project. Data warehouse and data mining applications, as already pointed out, support and facilitate all activities concerning the CRM, but they cannot guarantee complete organizational and operational market change. These technologies are means adapted by middle management to enter or capture a new market or consolidate the existing one. They make it possible, in fact, to emphasize the positive features of the company, of the customer and of their reciprocal relationship.

The last consideration concerns the role that human resources play in these contexts. Starting from the main objective of continually offering the client something better, we have already pointed out that this can be possible when even the employees are able to change their approach to the clients who are the targets of their work. In this regard, relationships are the area most involved. Companies that own a CRM structure must bear this in mind when selecting their personnel. They must in fact choose the right people and train them accurately to ensure they will be able to maintain and manage relationships with customers.

9.5   Critical Success Factors

The case studies analysed in the book have a mutual genesis: every successful case refers to a company that realized it was no longer able to anticipate and actively fulfil its customers' needs. Therefore, it was decided that a customer relationship management project should be implemented.

The thesis behind this conclusion is that the seeds of success in these experiences were sown during the worst and most difficult period and that success depends directly on the project plan. In these circumstances the enterprises analysed were able to understand and delineate the problematic features; they considered different solutions and accepted further economic effort and organizational changes in order to get over the crisis once and for all. A nonordered and necessarily partial list of the most delicate aspects and of the most effective internal levers to be considered when a CRM project is to be implemented is given below:

1. Project length,
2. The role played by external consultants,
3. The right weight given to technologies,
4. New internal skills,
5. New responsibilities of employees relationships between business functions,
6. Change in work processes the required cultural change,
7. Role played by business sponsors,

8. Cost of organizational and human resources,

9. Steps in the change process,

10. Team in charge of supervising the project,

11. Economic justification for the project,

12. Internal commitment to be developed,

13. Project leadership,

14. Change in behaviour toward the customers,

15. Staff training programme management of internal resistance to change,

16. Objectives to be reached.

Companies that considered and tackled these aspects and immediately faced up to them were then able to rise to the challenge and win through by adapting CRM solutions.

References

Adriaans P., Zantinge D. (1996): *Data Mining*, Addison-Wesley, Harlow.

Aha D.W., Kibler D., Albert M.K. (1991): *Instance Based Learning Algorithms*, in *Machine Learning*, n. 6, Kluwer Academic Publishers, Dordrecht.

Allen B. (1987): *Making Information Services Pay its Way*, Harvard Business Review, January-February.

Allen B.P. (1994): *Case Based Reasoning: Business Applications*, in *Communications of the ACM*, Vol. 37, Issue 3.

Angel B. (2000): *CRM: The Upgrade*, Canadian Banker, Third Quarter, Vol. 107, Issue 3.

Angell I., Smithson S. (1992): *Information Systems Management*, Mac Millan, London.

Anthony R.N. (1965): *Planning and Control System: a Framework for Analysis*, Harvard University Press, Cambridge.

Arthur B., Holland J., Palmer R., Tayler P. (1991): *Using Genetic Algorithms to Model the Stockmarket*, in *Proceedings of the Forecasting and the Optimisation in Financial Services Conference*, IBC Technical Services Ltd.

Associazione Bancaria Italiana (2000): *Rilevazione dello stato dell'automazione del sistema creditizio*, July, Roma.

Avison D. (1993): *Information Systems Development: A Database Approach*, A. Wallwer Ltd., Southampton.

Avison D., Fitzgerald G. (1996): *Information Systems Development: Methodologies, Techniques and Tools*, 2nd edition, McGraw-Hill, London.

Avison D., Horton J. (1993): *Evaluation and Information Systems Development*, in Arduini R. (edited by), *Investimenti in Information Technology nel settore bancario*, FrancoAngeli, Milano.

Bach D. (2001): *Do Online Banks Need CRM?*, American Banker, 30 April Supplement, Vol. 166, Issue 82.

Baestaens D.E. et al. (1994): *Neural Network Solutions for Trading in Financial Markets*, The Financial Times, Pitman Publishing, London.

Banca d'Italia (1996): *Tematiche aziendali: la tecnologia dell'informazione e la Banca d'Italia*, 2nd edition, November.

Baravelli M. (1984): *Politiche di automazione e home banking: prospettive per le banche italiane*, in Banche e Banchieri, n.9.

Baravelli M. (1988): *Strategie bancarie e politiche di automazione: profili gestionali ed organizzativi*, in Il Risparmio, March/April.

Barrett S. et al. (1982): *Interorganizational Information Sharing Systems*, in MIS Quarterly, Special Issue.

Barrow D. (1992): *Making Money with Genetic Algorithms*, In *Proceedings of the Fifth European Seminar on Neural Network and Genetic Algorithms*, IBC international services.

Bashford S. (2001): *HBOS awards CRM Role to Norwich Union Boss*, Marketing, 29 November, UK.

Belking N.J., Croft W.B. (1992): *Information Filtering and Information Retrieval: Two Sides of The Same Coin*, in Communication of ACM, Vol. 35, Issue 12.

Bello M. (2000): *Applicazioni di Data Mining a supporto della funzione marketing: l'esperienza di Banca Monte dei Paschi di Siena*, in Rajola F. (edited by), *L'organizzazione dei sistemi di Business Intelligence nel settore finanziario*, FrancoAngeli, Milano.

Benjamin R.I., Rockart J.F., Scott M.M.S., Wyman J. (1984): *Information Technology: a Strategic Opportunity*, in Sloan Management Review, Spring.

Bennett R.A. (2002): *How Not to Win Friends*, S. Banker, May, Vol. 112, Issue 5.

Berry L. L. (1983): *Relationship Marketing*, American Marketing Association.

Berry M., Linoff G. (1997): *Data Mining Techniques*, John Wiley & Sons, New York.

Berry M., Linoff G. (1999): *Mastering Data Mining: The Art and Science of Customer Relationship Management*, John Wiley & Sons, New York.

Berson A., Smith S., Thearling K. (2000): *Building Data Mining Applications for CRM*, Datamanagement, Osborne, McGraw-Hill, USA.

Bielski L. (2000): *Behavior Driven CRM*, ABA Banking Journal, October, Vol. 92, Issue 10.

Bielski L. (2001): *Giving Your Customer a Face*, ABA Banking Journal, April, Vol. 93, Issue 4.

Blattberg R., Getz G., Thomas J.S. (2001): *Customer Equity: Building and Managing Relationship as Valuable Assets*, HBS Press Book.

Bodega D. (1997): *L'adhocrazia*, in Costa C., Nacamulli M. (edited by), *Manuale di organizzazione aziendale. La progettazione organizzativa*, Vol. 2, Utet, Torino.

Bolman L.G., Deal T.E. (1997): *Reframing Organizations*, Jossey-Bass Publishers, San Francisco.

Bottiglia R. (1989): *La presenza bancaria nelle società di servizi informatici: obiettivi e modelli di intervento*, in Bottiglia R., De Laurentis G., Previati D. (edited by), *Banca e tecnologia: l'information technology come vantaggio competitivo*, Egea, Newfin, Milano.

Bracchi G., Motta G. (1988): *Progetto di sistemi informativi*, FrancoAngeli, Milano.

Branchman R.J., Anand T. (1996): *The Process of Knowledge Discovery in Databases: A Human-Centered Approach*, in Fayyad U. M., Shapiro G. (edited by), *Advances in Knowledge Discovery and Data Mining*, AAAI - Mit Press, Cambridge, Massachusetts.

Breiman L., Friedman J.H., Olshen R.A., Stone C.J. (1984): *Classification and Regression Trees*, Wadsworth Inc., Bertmon, CA.

Brown S.A. (1999): *Strategic Customer Care*, John Wiley & Sons, New York.

Brown S.A. (2000): *Customer Relationship Management: Linking People, Process and Technology*, John Wiley & Sons, New York.

Brown S.A. (2000): *Customer Relationship Management: A Strategic Imperative in the World of e-Business*, John Wiley & Sons, Etobicoke.

Burn J.M. (1989): *The Impact of Information Technology on Organisational Structures*, in Information & Management, n. 16, Elsevier Science Publishers, Holland.

Burnett K. (2001): *The Handbook of Key Customer Relationship Management – The Definitive Guide to Winning, Managing and Developing Key Account Business*, Financial Times, Prentice Hall, London.

Burns T., Stalker G.M. (1961): *The Management of Innovation*, Tavistock Pubblications, London.

Busch E.A., Jarvenpaa S.L., Tractinsky N., Glick W.H. (1991): *External Versus Internal Perspective in Determining a Firm's Progressive Use of Informa-*

tion Technology, in *Proceedings of the 12th International Conference on Information Systems*, New York.

Cantone A.N. (1996): *Creazione di valore attraverso le relazioni con i clienti*, ESI, Milano.

Camuffo A., Costa G. (1995): *Banca & organizzazione*, Edibank, Milano.

Carignani A., Mandelli A. (edited by) (1999): *Fare Business in Rete*, McGraw-Hill, Milano.

Carignani A. (2001): *Mobile Commerce: tecnologie, falsi miti e opportunità*, in Carignani A., Sorrentino M. (edited by), *On-line Banking*, McGraw-Hill, Milano.

Carignani A. (2001): *Pensare ed organizzare la banca diretta: stato dell'arte e scenari sul mercato europeo*, in Resti A. (edited by), (2001), *Banca virtuale e multicanale*, Edibank, Roma.

Carlzon J. (1991): *La piramide rovesciata*, FrancoAngeli, Milano.

Cash J.I., McFarlan W.F., McKenney J.L. (1988): *Corporate Information Systems Management*, Irwin, Homewood, Illinois.

Cesarini F. (1995): *La banca come impresa concorrenziale: alcune riflessioni*, in Banca Notizie, January, n.1.

Chablo E. (1999): *The Importance of Marketing Data Intelligence in Delivering Successful CRM*, SmartFOCUS.

Child J. (1987): *Information Technology, Organization and Response to Strategic Challenges*, in California Management Review.

Child J. (1988): *Tecnologia dell'informazione e reti di impresa*, in Sviluppo e Organizzazione, May/June, n.107.

Ciborra C. et al. (1978): *Management and Computers*, IFIP World Conference Proceedings.

Ciborra C. et al. (edited by) (1978): *Informatica e organizzazione*, FrancoAngeli, Milano.

Ciborra C. (1989): *Tecnologie di coordinamento*, FrancoAngeli, Milano.

Ciborra C. (1993): *Teams, Markets and Systems*, Cambridge University Press, Cambridge.

Ciborra C., Jelassi T. (edited by) (1994): *Strategic Information Systems - a European Perspective*, John Wiley & Sons, New York.

Ciborra C. (1999): *Notes on Improvisation and Time in Organizations*, Journal of Accounting, Management and Information Technologies, Volume 9, Issue 2, April.

Ciborra C. (edited by) (1996): *Groupware and Teamwork*, John Wiley & Sons, New York.

Ciborra C., Pugliese S. (1997): *La tecnologia*, in Costa C., Nacamulli M. (edited by), *Manuale di organizzazione aziendale. La progettazione organizzativa*, Vol. 2, Utet, Torino.

Ciborra C. (1998): *Teams, Markets and Systems*, Cambridge University Press, Cambridge.

Ciborra C. (edited by) (2000): *From Control to Drift: the Dynamics of Corporate Information Infastructures*, Oxford University Press, Oxford.

Cioccarelli G. (1991): *La prospettiva organizzativa nella progettazione del sistema informativo*, in Cioccarelli G. (edited by), *Progettazione organizzativa e sistema informativo nelle aziende di credito*, Giuffrè, Milano.

CIPA/ABI (1999): *Rilevazione dello stato dell'automazione del sistema creditizio*.

Clifton H.D. (1990): *Business Data Systems*, Prentice Hall, London.

Coffey J. O'Brien (2001): *The Road to CRM Nirvana. Bank Systems & Technology*, July, Vol. 38, Issue 7.

Costa C., Nacamulli M. (edited by) (1997): *Manuale di organizzazione aziendale. Le teorie dell'organizzazione*, Vol. 1, Utet, Torino.

Costa C., Nacamulli M. (edited by) (1997): *Manuale di organizzazione aziendale. La progettazione organizzativa*, Vol. 2, Utet, Torino.

Costa C., Nacamulli M. (edited by) (1997): *Manuale di organizzazione aziendale. I processi, i sistemi e le funzioni aziendali*, Vol. 3, Utet, Torino.

Costa C., Nacamulli M. (edited by) (1997): *Manuale di organizzazione aziendale. Metodi e tecniche di analisi e di intervento*, Vol. 5, Utet, Torino.

Cranford S. (1998): *Knowledge through DWH: DM, the Intelligent Component*, DM Review, May, www.dmreview.com.

Cuomo M. T. (2000): *La Customer Satisfaction*, Cedam, Padova.

Currie W., Galliers B. (edited by) (1999): *Rethinking Management Information Systems*, Oxford University Press, Oxford.

Daft R.L. (2000), *Organization Theory and Design*, (7th ed.), South-Western Thompson Learning.

Dayhoff J. (1990): *Neural Network Architectures: an Introduction*, Van Nostrand Reinhold, New York

De Maio A. (1971): *L'approccio per sistemi nelle organizzazioni*, in *Studi organizzativi*, n.3.

De Marco M. (1976): *I sistemi informativi*, FrancoAngeli, Milano.

De Marco M. (1988): *Aspettative e realtà dell'intelligenza artificiale*, in *Aggiornamenti Sociali*, n.11.

De Marco M. (1991): *Integrazione di sistemi esperti con il sistema informativo bancario*, in Gardin F., Rossignoli C., Vaturi S., *Sistemi esperti banca e finanza*, il Mulino, Bologna.

De Marco M. (1991): *Tendenze dell'innovazione tecnologica nel settore creditizio*, in Cioccarelli G. (edited by), *Progettazione organizzativa e sistema informativo nelle aziende di credito*, Giuffrè, Milano.

De Marco M. (1992): *I sistemi informativi*, in De Marco M., Bruschi G., Manna E., Giustiniani G., Rossignoli C. *L'organizzazione dei sistemi informativi aziendali*, Il Mulino, Bologna.

De Marco M. (1992): *L'organizzazione dei sistemi informativi aziendali*, Il Mulino, Bologna.

De Marco M. (1993): *Performance Evalutation e Capacity Planning dello sportello bancario: origini, motivazioni e tecniche*, in Arduini R. (edited by), *Investimenti in Information Technology nel settore bancario*, FrancoAngeli, Milano.

De Marco M. (1997): *Ruolo, prospettive e applicazioni dell'intelligenza artificiale nel mondo finanziario*, in *Volume di Economia e Finanza Aziendale*, Scritti in onore di Edoardo Ardemani, Giuffrè, Milano.

De Marco M. (2002): *I sistemi informativi aziendali. Temi di attualità*, FrancoAngeli, Milano.

Dearden J. (1987): *The Withering Away of the IS Organization*, Sloan Management Review, Summer.

Dearden J., Nolan R. (1973): *How to Control the Computer Resource*, Harvard Business Review, November/December.

Deboeck G. J. (edited by) (1995): *Trading on the Edge*, John Wiley & Sons, New York.

Decastri M. (1984): *Organizzazione e cultura dell'innovazione in impresa*, Giuffrè, Milano.

Decastri M., De Marco M., Rajola F. (2001): *Processi decisionali e flessibilità: il customer relationship management in banca*, in Giovanni Costa (edited by), *Flessibilità e Performance – L'organizzazione aziendale tra old e new economy*, Isedi, Torino.

Del Ciello N., Dulli S., Saccardi A. (2000): *Metodi di data mining per il customer relationship management*, FrancoAngeli, Milano.

Delmater R., Hancok M. (2001): *Data Mining Explained – A Manager's Guide to Customer Centric Business Intelligence*, Digital Press, Woburn, USA.

Devecchi C., Grandori A. (1993): *I processi decisionali d'impresa. La scelta dei sistemi informativi*, Giuffrè, Milano.

Drucker F. P. (1973): *Management: Tasks, Responsibilities, Practises*, Harper & Row, New York.

Dubois D., Prada H. (1980): *Fuzzy Sets and Systems: Theory and Application*, Academic Press, San Diego.

Dyché J. (2000): *e-Data: Turning Data into Information with Data Warehousing*, Addison-Wesley, Boston.

Eager A. (2001): *Marketing Manoeuvres*, Computer Business Review, November, Vol. 9, Issue 11.

Earl M.J. (1989): *Management Strategies for Information Management*, Prentice Hall, London.

Earl M.J. (1996): *The Risk of IT Outsourcing*, in Sloan Management Review, Vol. 37, Issue 3.

Earl M.J. (edited by) (1988): *Information Management: the Strategic Dimension*, Clarendon Press, Oxford.

Edelstein H. (2000): *Building Profitable Customer Relationships with Data Mining*, SPSS, White Paper.

Egan N.T. (1999): *Making a Successful CRM Transformation*, U.S. Banker, September, Vol. 109, Issue 9.

Eilon J. J. (2001): *Looking for Payback from CRM*, Bank Technology News, June, Vol. 14, Issue 6.

Evernden R. (1996): *The Information Framework*, in IBM System Journal, Vol. 35, n.1.

Fayyad U. M., Shapiro G. (edited by) (1996): *Advances in Knowledge Discovery and Data Mining*, AAAI - Mit Press, Cambridge, Massachusetts.

Feeny D., Earl M., Edwards B. (1987): *Organizational Arrangements for IS Roles of Users and IS Specialists*, Research and Discussion Paper RPD 94/6, Oxford Institute of Information Management, Templeton College, Oxford.

Feeny D.F., Willcocks L. (1997): *Managing Strategic Technology Projects. Key Trends: Capabilities and Learning*, in Willcocks L., Feeny D.F., Islei G., *Managing IT as a Strategic Resource*, McGraw-Hill, Cambridge.

Feigenbaum A. (1983): *Total Quality Control*, McGraw-Hill, New York.

Fontana F. (1995): *Il sistema organizzativo aziendale*, FrancoAngeli, Milano.

Fontana F. (1997): *La formulazione delle strategie*, in Costa C., Nacamulli M. (edited by), *Manuale di organizzazione aziendale. I processi, i sistemi e le funzioni aziendali*, Vol. 3, Utet, Torino.

Forslund M. (1999): *Creating a Direction in the Organisation*, Vaxjo University Press, Vaxio, Sweden.

Frawley W.J., Shapiro G.P., Matheus J.C. (1991): *Knowledge Discovery in Databases: An Overview*, AAAI Press, Menlo Park, CA.

Free D., Close W., Eisenfeld B., De Lotto R. (2001): *Can FSPs Gain Benefits From CRM?*, Gartner Group, Stamford.

Freeman A. (1996): *It's Consumer Banking*, Economist, 26 October, Technology in finance, Vol. 341, Issue 7989.

Galbraith J.R. (1977): *Organization Design*, Addison-Wesley, Menlo Park, CA.

Galliers R.D., Baets W.R.J. (edited by) (2000): *Information Technology and Organizational Transformation – Innovation for the 21st Century Organization*, in Wiley Series in Information System, John Wiley & Sons, Chichester, England.

Gilmore J.H., Pine B.J. II (edited with an introduction by) (2000): *Markets of One – Creating Customer-Unique Value through Mass Customization*, A Harvard Business Review Book, Harvard.

Goldberg D.E. (1989): *Genetic Algorithms in Search Optimization and Machine Learning*, Addison-Wesley, Menlo Park, CA.

Golden J. (1993): *Economics and National Strategy: Convergence, Global Networks, and Cooperative Competition*, The Washington Quarterly, Summer.

Goldman L.F. (2001): *CRM: Anatomy of a DWH Failure*, DM Review Online, February, www.dmreview.com.

Golembiewski R.T. (1993): *Handbook of Organizational Behaviour*, Dekker Inc., New York.

Gostick R. (2000): *CRM is Dead, Long Live e-CRM*, Banker, July, Vol. 150, Issue 893.

Gotta M. (2000): *Managing the Point of Interaction*, META Group, Stamford.

Grandori A. (1988): *L'analisi dei costi per la progettazione organizzativa*, in *Sviluppo e Organizzazione*, January/February, n.105, Este, Milano.

Grandori A. (1989): *Rockart e Short sulla TI*, in *Sviluppo e Organizzazione*, September/October, n.115.

Griffin J. (1997): *Customer Loyalty*, Jossey-Bass Publisher, New York.

Grindley K. (1995): *Managing IT at Board Level*, 2nd ed., Pitman Publishing, London.

Groenfeldt T. (2000): *Customer Data, Tight Here, Right Now*, U.S. Banker, May, Vol. 110, Issue 5.

Groenroos C. (1990): *Service Management and Marketing: Managing the Moments of Truth in Service Competition*, Lexington Books.

Groth R. (1998): *Data Mining. A Hands-on Approach for Business Professionals*, Prentice Hall PTR, Santa Clara, CA.

Hall R. (2001): *The New Revenue Model for CRM*, Bank Marketing, June, Vol. 33, Issue 5.

Hall R.E. (1999): *Relationship Data Won't Interpret Itself*, American Banker, 30 July, Vol. 164, Issue 145.

Hamblen M, (2000): *Instant Customer Data Gives Bank Sales Force an Edge*, Computerworld, 15 May, Vol. 34, Issue 20.

Hamil J. (2000): *Internet Supported CRM*, Discussion Paper, www.crm-forum.com.

Hammer M. (1990): *Re-engineering Work: Don't Automate, Obliterate*, Harvard Business Review, September/October.

Holland J.H. (1973): *Genetic Algorithms and the Optimal Allocations of the Trials*, in SIAM Journal of Computing, n. 2.

Holland J.H. (1984): *Genetic Algorithms and Adaptation*, in Selfridge O.G., *Proceedings of the NATO Advanced Research Institute on Adaptive Control of Systems*, Plenum Press.

Holland J.H. (1987): *Genetic Algorithms and Classifier Systems: Foundations and Future Directions*, in Grefenstette J.J. (edited by), *Genetic Algorithms and their Applications: Proceedings of the Second International Conference on Genetic Algorithms*, Lawrence Erlbaum Associates, London.

Holland J.H. (1993): *Adaption in Natural and Artificial Systems*, Mit Press, Cambridge, Massachusetts.

Holland J.H. (1993): *Genetic Algorithms and the Optimal Allocations of Trials*, in SIAM Journal of computing, n. 2, 1973.

Iivari J. (1992): *The Organisational Fit of Information Systems*, in Journal of Information Systems, n. 2.

Imhoff C., Loftis L., Geiger J.G., foreword by Inmon W. H. (2001): *Building the Customer-Centric Enterprise – Data Warehousing Techniques for Supporting Customer Relationship Management*, John Wiley & Sons, Canada.

Inmon W.H. (1996): *Building the Data Warehouse*, 2nd ed., John Wiley & Sons, New York.

Juran J.M. (1964): *Managerial Breakthrough*, McGraw-Hill, New York.

Keen P., Scott M.M.S. (1978): *Decision Support Systems: an Organizational Perspective*, Addison-Wesley, Massachusetts.

Keen P. (1981): *Information Systems and Organizational Change*, in Communications of the ACM, Vol.. 24, Issue 1.

Keen P. (1988): *Rebuilding the Human Resources of Information Systems*, Earl M. (edited by), *Information Management. The Strategic Dimension*, Clarendon Press, Oxford.

Keenan C. (2001): *Translating Customer Service to the Front Lines*, American Banker, 7 May, Vol. 166, Issue 87.

Keene R. (2001): *CRM's Value Can Be Found In Improved Customer Loyalty*, American Banker, 10 October, Vol. 166, Issue 196.

Kelly S. (1997): *Data Warehousing in Action*, John Wiley & Sons, New York.

Kiesnoski K. (1999): *Customer Relationship Management*, (cover story) Bank Systems & Technology, February, Vol. 36, Issue 2.

Kimball R. (1996): *Data Warehouse Toolkit*, John Wiley & Sons, New York.

Kingdon J., Feldman K. (1995): *Intelligent Techniques Applied in Finance*, in Nottola C., Rossignoli C. (edited by), *Intelligenza artificiale in banca: tendenze evolutive ed esperienze operative a confronto*, FrancoAngeli, Milano.

Kirkpatrick S., Gelatt C.D. (1983): *Optimization by Simulated Annealing*, in Science, n. 22.

Kohonen T. (1990): *The Self-Organizing Map, Proceedings of IEEE Conference*.

Kolodner J. (1991): *Improving Human Decision Making Through Case Based Decision Aiding*, in A.I. Magazine, Vol. 12 n.2.

Kosko B. (1992): *Neural Networks and Fuzzy Systems. A Dynamical Systems Approach to Machine Intelligence*, Prentice-Hall, Englewood Cliffs, New Jersey.

Kosko B. (1996): *Fuzzy Engineering*, Prentice-Hall, Englewood Cliffs, New Jersey.

Kotler P. (1999): *Kotler on Marketing: How to Create, Win and Dominate Markets*, Free Press, New York.

Kotler P., Scott W. G. (1997): *Marketing Management*, Isedi, Torino.

Lawrence P., Lorsch I. (1967): *Organizations and Environment*, Harvard Business Press, Cambridge.

Lee D. (2000): *The Customer Relationship Management Planning Guide V2.0: CRM Steps I & II, Customer-Centric Planning & Redesigning Roles*, High-Yield Marketing Press, Heinel Drive MN.

Levitt I. (1969): *The Marketing Mode: Pathways to Corporate Growth*, McGraw-Hill, New York.

Lucas H.C. (1984): *Organizational Power and the Information Service Department*, in Communications of the ACM, Vol.27, Issue 1.

Lucas H.C. (1992): *The Analysis, Design and Implementation of Information Systems*, McGraw-Hill, New York.

Maggi B. (edited by) (Italian Edition) (1989): *L'azione organizzativa*, Isedi, Torino. (Thompson J.D., (1967), *Organizations in Action*, McGraw-Hill).

Mandujano M. (2000): *The Latin American CRM Banks*, Bank Technology News, November, Vol. 13, Issue 11.

March J.G., Cyert R.M. (1963): *A Behavioural Theory of the Firm*, Prentice Hall, New Jersey.

Maselli J. (2001): *Industry-Tuned CRM Suites Save Time*, InformationWeek, 5 November, Issue 862.

Maslow A. (1964): *Motivation and Personality*, Harper & Row, New York.

Mayes N. (2001): *Banks Still Keen on CRM and Outsourcing*, Global Computing Services, 5 October.

McDonald M., Rogers B. (1999): *La gestione dei clienti strategici*, FrancoAngeli, Milano.

McFarlan F.W., McKenney J.L. (1983): *Corporate Information Systems Management: the Issue Facing Senior Management*, Irwin Inc. Homewood.

McFarlan F.W., Nolan R.L. (1995): *How to Manage an IT Outsourcing Alliance*, Sloan Management Review, Winter.

McKeen J.D., Smith H.A. (1996): *Management Challenges in IS: Successful Strategies and Appropriate Action*, John Wiley & Sons, Chichester.

McKenna R. (1993): *Relationship Marketing: Successful Strategies for the Age of the Customer*, Addison-Wesley, Boston.

Mercurio R., De Vita P. (1997): *Il marketing e la commercializzazione*, in Costa G., Nacamulli R. (edited by) *Manuale di organizzazione aziendale. I processi, i sistemi e le funzioni aziendali*, Vol. 3, Utet, Torino.

META Group (1996): *Marketing IT*, Advanced Information Management Strategies - AIMS, Stamford.

META Group (1996): *Service & Systems Management Strategies: The Business of IT*, SSMS, Stamford.

META Group (1997): *The New IT Professionals*, META Group, Stamford.

META Group (2000): *Leadership Strategies in Customer Relationship Management*, Stamford.

Miles R.E., Snow C.C. (1996): *The Network Firm: a Spherical Structure Built on a Human Investment Philosophy*, Haas School of Business, Berkeley.

Miles R.H. (1980): *Macro Organizational Behaviour*, Goodyear Publishing Company, Santa Monica.

Mintzberg H. (1979): *The Structuring of Organizations*, Prentice Hall, New Jersey.

Mintzberg H. (1983): *Designing Effective Organizations*, Prentice Hall, New Jersey.

Mintzberg H. (1985): *Structures in Fives. Designing Effective Organizations*, Prentice Hall, New Jersey. (Italian translation, *La progettazione dell'organizzazione aziendale*, il Mulino, Bologna).

Morris G. (2002): *Beyond CRM: Assessing Clients' Value*, Bank Investment Marketing, February, Vol. 10, Issue 2.

Morse S., Isaac D. (1998): *Parallel Systems in the Data Warehouse*, Prentice Hall, New Jersey.

Nadin G., Cerri A. (1999): *Call Center e CRM*, in Sistemi & Impresa, n.10, December.

Nadin G. (2000): *Customer Relationship Management: fidelizzazione clienti e reddito d'impresa*, in Amministrazione & Finanza, n.1.

Newell F. (2000): *Loyalty.com*, McGraw-Hill, New York.

Normann R. (1985): *La gestione strategica dei servizi*, EtasLibri, Milano.

Nottola C. Rossignoli C. (edited by) (1994): *Analisi della esperienza operativa sull'utilizzo dell' intelligenza artificiale in banca*, FrancoAngeli, Milano.

Nottola C., Rossignoli C. (edited by) (1995): *Intelligenza artificiale in banca: tendenze evolutive ed esperienze operative a confronto*, FrancoAngeli, Milano.

Oliver R. L. (1997): *Satisfaction*, McGraw-Hill, New York.

Optner Stanford L. (1965): *System Analysis for Business and Industrial Problem Solving*, Prentice-Hall, Englewood Cliff, New Jersey.

Österle H. et al. (1994): *Business Process Monitoring*, in *Proceedings of the Second Conference on Information Systems*, Nijenrode University, Nijenrode University Press.

Österle H. (1995): *Business in the Information Age. Heading for New Processes*, Springer, Berlin.

Patterson T.D. (2000): *Data Mining for Golden Opportunities*, Computing: 50 hot technologies, Vol.8 Issue 1, January, www.datamininglab.com.

Pavia J. (1999): *Just Thinking...* , Bank System & Technology, April, Vol. 36, Issue 4.

Peppers D., Rogers M. (1997): *The One to One Future: Building Relationships One Customers at a Time*, Currency Doubleday, New York.

Peppers D., Rogers M., Dorf B. (1998): *Enterprise One to One: Tools for Competing in the Interactive Age*, Doubleday, New York.

Perrone V. (1990): *Le strutture organizzative d'impresa. Criteri e modelli di progettazione*, Egea, Milano.

Petersen G.S. (1997): *High-Impact Sales Force Automation: A Strategic Perspective*, CRC Press - St. Lucie Press.

Poe V. (1996): *Building a Data Warehouse for Decision Support,* Prentice-Hall, Englewood Cliffs, New Jersey.

Pontiggia A. (1992): *L'evoluzione organizzativa delle reti di sportelli bancari*, in Sviluppo e Organizzazione, n. 129, January/February.

Porter M.E., Millar V.E. (1985): *How Information Gives You Competitive Advantages*, Harvard Business Review, July/August.

Pricewaterhouse-Coopers Consulting (2000), *Il manuale per la gestione della relazione con il cliente.*

Ptacek M. J. (2000): *Search for Perfect CRM Solution Remains Elusive*, American Banker, 9 September, Vol. 165, Issue 173.

Ptacek M.J. (2000): *What is CRM? Proponents Say Wall Street May Insist that Banks Know*, American Banker, 10 October, Vol. 165, Issue 90.

Ptacek M.J. (2001): *Banks Target CRM at Corporate Clients*, American Banker, 30 April Supplement, Vol. 166, Issue 82.

Puccinelli B. (1999): *Bank Delivery, Service Channels Require More Personal Attention*, Bank Systems & Technology, July, Vol. 36, Issue 7.

Quinlan J.R. (1986): *Introduction of Decision Trees*, Machine Learning, n.1.

Rajola F. (1999): *L'organizzazione della funzione sistemi informativi in banca*, FrancoAngeli, Milano.

Rajola F. (edited by) (2000): *L'organizzazione dei sistemi di Business Intelligence nel settore finanziario*, FrancoAngeli, Milano.

Rajola F. (2002): *Sistemi di CRM e Business Intelligence nel settore finanziario*, FrancoAngeli, Milano.

Riadon E.E., Bacon L.D. (1998): *DWH and DM: Possibilities Pitfalls, and Implications for Marketing Management and Research*, Georgia State University, www.marketing.gsu.edu.

Richmond W.B., Seidmann A., Whinston A.B. (1992): *Incomplete Contracting Issues in Information Systems Development Outsourcing*, Decision Support Systems, Vol. 8, n.5.

Riesback C.K. (1998): *An interface for Case Based Knowledge Acquisition*, in *Proceedings of the DARPA Workshop on Case Based Reasoning*, DARPA, Arlington VA.

Rigby D.K., Reichheld F. F., Schefter P. (2002): *Avoid the Four Perils of CRM*, Harvard Business Review, February, Vol. 80, Issue 2.

Rockart J.F. (1979): *Chief Executives Define Their Own Data Needs*, in Harvard Business Review, March/April.

Rockart J.F. (1988): *The Line Takes the Leadership - IS Management in a Wired Society*, in Sloan Management Review, Summer.

Roethlisberger F.J., Dickson W.J. (1939): *Management and the Worker*, Harvard University Press, Cambridge.

Rosander M. (1985): *Applications of Quality Control in Service Industries*, ASQC, Milwaukee.

Rossignoli C. (1993): *Applicazioni di sistemi esperti e reti neurali un campo finanziario*, FrancoAngeli, Milano.

Rossignoli C. (1997): *Organizzazione e sistemi informativi*, FrancoAngeli, Milano.

Rountree D. (2001): *Customers Rule Today*, (cover story) Bank Technology News, April, Vol. 14, Issue 4.

Rountree D. (2001): *Small Banks Move Toward CRM One Step At A Time*, Bank Technology News, April, Vol. 14, Issue 4.

Rountree D. (2002): *Data Management Boasts Major Role in Profitability*, Bank Technology News, February, Vol. 15, Issue 2.

Rugiadini A. (1970): *I sistemi informativi d'impresa*, Giuffrè, Milano.

Rugiadini A. (1979): *Organizzazione d'impresa*, Giuffrè, Milano.

Rumhelhart D.E., McCleland J.L. (1986): *Parallel Distributed Processing: Explorations in the Microstructures of Cognition*, Mit Press, Cambridge, Massachusetts.

Salvemini S. (1988): *L'organizzazione dei processi di marketing: alcuni criteri per un assetto organizzativo efficiente*, in Studi in onore di Luigi Guatri, Bocconi Comunicazione, Milano.

Schneider M. (2001): *Dirty Secret of CRM: It's 20% Strategy, 80% Grunt Work*, American Banker, 24 August, Vol. 166, Issue 164.

SCN Education B.V. (edited by) (2001): *Customer Relationship Management – The Ultimate Guide to the Efficient Use of CRM*, Vieweg, Netherland.

Scott Tillett L. (2000): *Smaller Banks Taking Up CRM Challenge*, Bank Systems & Technology, December, Vol. 37, Issue 12.

Scott W.G. (1967): *Presentazione*, in Bertucci M., (1997), *Conoscere il cliente*, Edibank, Milano.

Selvin, Hanan C., Stuart A. (1966): *Data-Dredging Procedures in Survey Analysis*, The American Statistician, June, Vol. 20.

Seybold P. B., Marshak R.T. (1999): *Customers.com – How to Create a Profitable Business Strategy for the Internet*, Random House, Business Book, Third Impression, Australia.

Shahanamn E. (2000): *The Customer Relationship Management Ecosystem*, META Group, Stamford.

Shesbunoff A. (1999): *Winning CRM Strategies*, ABA Banking Journal, October, Vol. 91, Issue 10.

Simon H.A. (1957): *Models of Men. Social e Rational*, John Wiley & Sons, New York.

Simon A. (1998): *90 Days to the Data Mart*, John Winley & Sons, New York.

Smale B. (2000): *Turning CRM Theory into Action*, Banker, August, Vol. 150, Issue 894.

Sprague R.H., McNurlin B.C. (1993): *Information Systems Management in Practice*, Prentice Hall, New Jersey.

Stein J. (1991): *Neural Networks: from the Chalkboard to the Trading Room*, Trading Techniques, New York.

Steiner T.D., Teixeira D.B. (1990): *Technology in Banking: Creating Value and Destroying Profits*, Business One Irwin, Homewood.

Stone M., Woodcock N., Machtynger L. (2000): *Customer Relationship Marketing – Get to Know Your Customers and Win Their Loyalty*, Kogan Page, London.

Sweeney P. (2001): *Cutting Through the CRM Hype*, U.S. Banker, June, Vol. 111, Issue 6.

Tarun K. (1990): *Foundations of Neural Networks*, Addison-Wesley, New York.

Taylor F.W. (1911): *Scientific Management*, Harper & Row, New York.

Thompson J.D. (1967): *Organizations in Action*, McGraw-Hill, New York.

Tulley J. (2001): *Establishing Unique Customer Relations Using Data Warehousing*, (cover story) Canadian Manager, Spring, Vol. 26, Issue 1.

Turban E., Trippi R. (1993): *Neural Networks in Finance and Investing: Using Artificial Intelligence to Improve Real-World Performance*, Probus publishing company, New York.

Tynan T.G. (2000): *Web Adds Pressure for CRM*, American Banker, 20 April, Vol. 165, Issue 77.

Unwin C., Cogbill S. (1991): *Artificial Intelligence in Financial Trading*, Financial trading International, New York.

Valdani E. (1995): *Marketing strategico*, ETAS, Milano.

Valentine L. (1999): *First Union Tackles CRM with CRMs*, ABA Banking Journal, October, Vol. 91, Issue 10.

Valino J., Rubio R., Villaverde R.F. (1989): *Credit card Evaluation System Based on Neural Computing*, IDSIA, Lugano.

Varhol P.D. (1996): *Reengineering the Information Technology Organization*, Computer Technology Research Corp - CTR, Charleston.

Virtuani R. (1997): *L'outsourcing nei sistemi informativi aziendali*, FrancoAngeli, Milano.

Wasserman P.D. (1989): *Neural Computing: Theory and Practice*, Van Nostrand Reinhold, New York.

Weber M. (1922): *Wirtschaft und Gesellschaft*, Mohr, Tübingen.

West L. (2001): *Where's the Relationship in eCRM?*, Bank Technology News, April, Vol. 14, Issue 4.

Willcocks L., Feeny D.F., Islei G. (1997): *Managing IT as a Strategic Resource*, McGraw-Hill, Cambridge.

Williamson O.E. (1975): *Markets and Hierarchies*, Free Press, New York.

Williamson O.E. (1981): *The Economics of Organization: The Transaction Cost Approach*, American Journal of Sociology, Vol. 87, n. 3.

Winfield I. (1986): *Human Resources and Computing*, Heinemann, London.

Wu J. (2000): *Business Intelligence: What is Data Mining?*, DM Review Online, August, www.dmreview.com

Yasin R. (2001): *Banks Embrace CRM Technology*, InternetWeek, 26 March, Issue 854.

Young K. (1999): *Customer Care Centres on Profit*, American Banker, October, Vol. 149, Issue 884.

Young M.M. (2002): *Banking on CRM*, Intelligent Enterprise, 21 February, Vol. 5, Issue 4.

Yourdon E. (1989): *Modern Structured Analysis*, Prentice Hall, New Jersey.